I0622851

# AMERICAN CHRISTIANITY

*Black Liberation White Legalism*

## PASTOR OWEN E. WILLIAMS

AMERICAN CHRISTIANITY

Copyright © 2023 by Pastor Owen E. Williams

Cover Design: 99 Design by Vista

Author Photo: T. L. Holmes

Typesetting: Edge of Water Designs, edgeofwater.com

ISBNs:

   979-8-9874758-0-5 (Paperback)

   979-8-9874758-1-2 (Digital Online)

   979-8-9874758-2-9 (Hardback)

Publisher: Grapevine Publishing Press

# DEDICATION

Thank you to my life partner and wife for the last thirty-two years, Elder Debora Williams, for your love, support, and daily prayers over my life. She has been the lead servant for "Desire a Prayer Life Ministries" for the last twenty-two years. God has anointed Elder Debora with a ministry that allows her to bring the "Power of Prayer" back into the home and to help people develop a disciplined prayer life at www.desireaprayerlife.com. Through her insight and wisdom, she has been a bright guiding light in my life to my precious daughter, Desiree Rose Williams, who has grown up and matured into a beautiful and responsible young woman over the last decade. Your dad loves you and is immensely proud of you.

To the memories of my mother and father, I think about them every day.

# FOREWORD

Some may find it surprising to see a rabbi writing the foreword for Reverend Owen Williams' brave book on the nature of racism within the church. But the profound lessons that this book delivers transcend the religious divide. The book is an impassioned argument for taking inventory of past discriminatory attitudes and an opportunity for all institutions, and the people within them, to repent and improve.

The book provides a rich platform for any person of faith to measure their actions through their sense of their faith, religion, and scripture. Indeed, every person of faith must engage in reckoning with one's actions. This lesson is as important in Judaism as it is in Christianity.

We face many challenges these days, political, economic, environmental, and religious. We are constantly pushed to focus on what divides us. Reverend

Williams' book reminds us that all people of faith climb a metaphorical mountain. The climb and the path we choose are filled with challenges, successes, insights, and great teachers. At the base of the hill, the different camps may be so far apart that they are invisible. As we climb, the distances between us get shorter. The language becomes closer. At the summit, we communicate similar values: charity, activism, community, and protection of the weak, the vulnerable, and the poor. Close to the plateau, we espouse similar practices: prayer, commitment to action, mediation, learning, and growth.

The words of Reverend Williams connect our hearts, souls, and actions and unite us in a community of understanding.

Rabbi Igael Gurin-Malous is the founding rabbi and CEO of T'shuvah Center, an intentional spiritual healing community in NYC, and the host of Tattoos and Torah Podcast. He is a renowned Talmud teacher, spiritual counselor, artist, and educator who is often called upon to speak and write about modern spirituality,

Talmud, Jewish text, addiction, recovery, fatherhood, and LGBTQIA+ issues.

He worked at Beit T'Shuvah, the renowned residential recovery community in Los Angeles, first as a spiritual counselor and then as Director of Spiritual counseling. Since 2012, he has served as Temple Israel of Hollywood Talmud Scholar in Residence, teaching weekly classes on Interpreting Talmud. Rabbi Iggy serves on the board and faculty at the Academy of Jewish Religion of California (AJRCA).

# ACKNOWLEDGMENTS

I want to thank the following people, for this book would not be possible without its contributors.

To my Lord and Savior Jesus Christ, who kept me in my right mind through it all, has looked past all of my sins and faults and continues to pour out His divine will in my life.

To my beloved wife and life partner for the last thirty-two years, for her continued love, support, and encouragement.

To my daughter, you continue to make me the proudest dad on this side of heaven.

To my sister Susan Watkins, there is no better sister on this side of heaven. Thank you for all the love, phone calls, and retirement vision. I love you much.

To my mother and father, whom both have gone home to be with the Lord. Thank you for your trials and struggles in keeping the family together.

To the St. Mark Missionary Baptist Church, there is no finer place or more incredible people I would serve God with than you. God bless you.

To my sister and my nieces and nephew for their endless love.

The Professors and support staff at Liberty University Baptist Theological Seminary, yours is a mixture of grace, love, and knowledge. God Bless this great institution.

# PREFACE

This book attempts to understand and explain the churches' passive and, in some cases, silent national attitude and behavior towards matters of privilege, discrimination, greed, and racism towards Africans in and throughout the western world's history. We recognize that for too long, many marginalized people other than Africans have been affected by this sin of silence that has caused many good people of faith to ponder this same question while searching the Holy Scriptures for answers on salvation and deliverance. This book will attempt to seek truth in all of its rawness and discomfort as I address race relations in the west from the colonization of the Caribbean to the inception of America. We enter the second decade of the 21st century with an explosion of technological advances in medicine, communications, transportation, and space exploration. From the colonization of the stars to the architectural wonders on earth, our last frontier to explore and conquer is still the human heart and its propensity for great compassion and terrible atrocities. This next level of ministry will not be higher to mirror the times but deeper to connect and remind us of our humanity and the consequences of behavior.

# INTRODUCTION

Many Christians and non-Christians know and have opinions of the Christian faith and its central figure, "Jesus Christ." But how many know why the ecclesial body is the way it is and how Christ almost did not become our savior and central foundation of the faith? Theologians know this story well, but most laypeople will never go to seminary, and most non-accredited bible schools cannot afford to teach an in-depth curriculum. I do not present myself as a theologian nor a Biblical scholar, only as an ordained pastor who has been blessed to be guided by some brilliant and scholarly theologians when I went to seminary. There is a concrete reason for the trajectory and division of God's holy church, the behavior of its clergy, and the impotent reality of the body in today's society. Some may say we must not talk badly about the church in public, but I believe the church body is already talking and misbehaving for the world to see. In the third chapter of the book of Revelations, verses fourteen through nineteen, Christ revealed the character of today's church.

*"These things say the Amen, the Faithful and True Witness, the Beginning of the creation of God: "I know your works, that you are neither cold nor hot. I could wish you were cold or hot. So then, because you are lukewarm and neither cold nor hot, I will vomit you out of my mouth. Because you say, 'I am rich, have become wealthy, and require nothing and do not know that you are wretched, miserable, poor, blind, and naked. I counsel you to buy from Me gold refined in the fire, that you may be rich; and white garments, that you may be clothed, that the shame of your nakedness may not be revealed; and anoint your eyes with eye-salve, that you may see. As many as I love, I rebuke and chasten."*

This blind character is what I will attempt to explore in the upcoming chapters.

# TABLE OF CONTENTS

# Chapter 1

# CLIMATE OF MINISTRY

*2 Timothy 3: 1-5*

*But know this, that in the last days perilous times will come: for men will be lovers of themselves, lovers of money, boasters, proud, blasphemers, disobedient to parents, unthankful, unholy, unloving, unforgiving, slanderers, without self-control, brutal, despisers of good, traitors, headstrong, haughty, lovers of pleasure rather than lovers of God, having a form of godliness but denying its power. And from such people turn away!*

## A Penetrating Ethos

The Apostle Paul, in setting his spiritual son Timothy apart, forewarned and equipped him for the work that lay ahead. This work continues today, and the characteristics of the environments, cultures, industries, geographies, and professions remain the same. As the sixteenth century progressed, we saw an expansion of greed, lust, and cruelty grip the world; in this epoch, the following four hundred years changed the course of human history and ushered in ideologies and systems of classism, superiority, and inferiority complexes, and the official and legal government-approved racism and discrimination at pandemic levels that still profoundly affect every society on the planet. In the twenty-first century, we have seen this scripture in "Revelation 18: 1-3"

*"After these things I saw another angel coming down from heaven, having great authority, and the earth was illuminated with his glory. And he cried with a loud voice, saying, "Babylon the great is fallen, is fallen, and*

*has become a dwelling place of demons, a prison for every foul spirit, and a cage for every unclean and hated bird! For all the nations have drunk of the wine of the wrath of her fornication, the kings of the earth have committed fornication with her, and the merchants of the earth have become rich through the abundance of her luxury."*

Beginning to take shape throughout the world and was supported by the church. Ever since Emperor Constantine made the church the official religion of the Roman Empire and placed it in a position of privilege, the church abandoned its foundational doctrine of advocating for the poor, downtrodden, and motherless to adopt the new role of siding with the ruling class to keep its part of privilege in society. Even though a few local churches and denominations have returned to their foundational mandates, most still are more concerned with their positions and standings in society than the plight of the poor and oppressed. This attitude has only further widened the divide among the perceived united body of Christ, which has been divided socially, racially, financially, ethnically, and ethically.

## Sugar and Slavery

In the history of humanity, there has not been a natural resource that has caused more suffering to human society than sugar. As the European elite and the masses desire for the taste of sugar as a sweetener for coffee, tea, and chocolate increased, more secure sugarcane plantations and the controls over these plantations became an increasing priority. The plantations on the islands of Cyprus and the Mediterranean coast were controlled by the Byzantine Empire and were very expensive to import. With the discovery of the Caribbean and its rich and plentiful sugarcane plantations, European demand could finally be met at a lower cost. Sugar plantations are a very labor-intensive investment, so the need for massive investments in labor was essential to meet customers' demands. Since Europeans and Amerindians, who were the native peoples of the region, were regarded as weak and could not work in the hot and humid environments of the Caribbean plantations, Africans became the only choice. Enslaved Africans were transported across the Atlantic Ocean using Spanish and English slave ships. They began arriving in small numbers, and later the number increased. The highest forced migration from Africa to the West Indies was recorded between the sixteenth and nineteenth centuries. The foundational reason for this policy of African slavery was the skyrocketing profits of sugar sales to European society. In its many forms, sugar is as old as the earth; this sweet-tasting natural resource found a perfect home in human desire, not only in its taste but also through the complex process of harvesting and producing it. This commodity changed the lives and societies of the grower and those it was grown for. Even though the item of sugar was not a new thing, the sweetness of West Indies sugar cane transformed the world and left us with its present-day bitterness among the people of the world, including among the holy Congregations of the world. All because European society liked its sweet coffee, tea, and hot chocolate.

## Demand, Supply, Slavery

From the sixteenth to the nineteenth centuries, European entrepreneurs and aristocrats demanded this commodity, creating astronomical profits, unbridled greed, and extraordinary human atrocities worldwide. During this period, the British Empire exported hundreds of thousands of men, women, and children into the Caribbean islands of Jamaica, Trinidad, Surinam, Guyana, and Cuba. These were African slaves, Indian and Chinese indentured servants known by the derogatory racial term (Coolie). This displaced and enslaved workforce was gathered from around the globe for free and cheap labor, maximizing profits for sugar cane plantation owners. As the years passed and demands increased, sugar prices brought higher profit percentages, leading to exponential sugar cultivation and development growth. The commodity quickly became the number one trading item throughout the Caribbean and South America. This was a byproduct of an increased desire for sugar and sweetener throughout the European states. The discovery by the European industry that sugar could be used as an energy stimulant further increased demand as companies looked for competitive advantages to increase productivity. This led to a request to expand sugar plantations in the Caribbean and South Americas. This dynamic highlighted the plantation's labor problems and the need for a more stable and energetic workforce. Europeans and Amerindians were regarded as weak and unreliable for the heavy toll plantation work demanded, so Africans became the only labor of choice.

## Apostolic Era: The Logos of God

The apostolic era is the period from the start of Christ's ministry to the death of the last apostle. It's responsible for forming the Christian faith and followed by the sub-apostolic era. The apostolic age is all about building the Christian faith through the teachings of Jesus Christ *(John 1:1 "In the beginning was the word, and the word was with God, and the Word was God)."* To better understand this cosmic and biblical dynamic, the biblical definition of the word apostle is "one who is sent on a specific commission."

As Christ articulated in the twenty-eighth chapter of the gospel of Matthew: *"All authority in heaven and on earth has been given to me. Therefore, make disciples of all nations, baptizing them in the name of the Father, the Son, and the Holy Spirit and teaching them to obey everything I have commanded. And surely, I am with you always, to the very end of the age."*

To answer the multitude of questions about how the Christian faith began in nobility and strength of character to where it finds itself now requires an honest look back at our early infancy. We must look at both Christian history and ancient world history with a particular interest in the behavioral interactions between peoples, their customs, doctrines, and tribal cultures.

Because to see the actual characteristics of societies, we must look closely at their interpersonal relationships, laws, and class structure.

## Sub-Apostolic Era

This era of Christian history has been widely accepted, from the death of the Apostle John to the Nicaean council. This period is critical to shaping the characteristics of the church, its congregants, and the world itself. These times are the foundation of Paul's prophetic verse in second Timothy. Daniel's interpretation of King Nebuchadnezzar's dream is a wonderfully accurate picture of how the mixing of ideologies produced us. Daniel 2: 41, *"Whereas you saw the feet and toes, partly of potter's clay and partly of iron, the kingdom shall be divided; yet the strength of the iron shall be in it, just as you saw the iron mixed with ceramic clay."*

If anything, the last century has taught an age-old lesson that the state of man's relationships has always been and will continue to be built on a foundation of cantankerous behavior, divisive ideologies, and tenuous interest. The nineteenth century was a tough time for humanity. Yet, it provided great opportunities for Christians to practice their faith and exercise their gifts in mission work, witnessing, evangelizing, and church planting. And while some of those activities were done with great fanfare and hype from the Christian communities, they had minimal effect on stemming the tide of global corruption, war, and the inhumane and depraved policies of governments around the world. So as not to come across as naive, ignorant, or arrogant about the church, I am fully aware of the church's biblical boundaries in the world's political affairs but can't help but notice the disparity of involvement from international Christian bodies like the "World Council of Churches," the Vatican, and the Red Cross when it comes to leading the charge on matters of poverty and hunger but disappear when addressing the causes and catalysis for said problems when there is a clear, direct cause and effect between wars, civil wars, and government corruption to global poverty and hunger. The nineteenth century gave the world a lot of new theologies.

Still, the most dominant and prominent one as it pertained to the oppression of people came out of South America by Catholic priest Gustavo Gutierrez, and Jesuits Juan Luis Segundo and Jon Sobrino, called "Liberation Theology," which focuses emphasis on oppressed people in socioeconomic conditions of poverty, human rights, education, and addresses inequalities of race, class, and caste. The "Second Vatican Council" in the 1960s gave us ecumenical bodies worldwide addressing these conditions. In America, Professor James Cone of Union Theological Seminary penned "Black Liberation Theology." Even though it was not connected to the American Civil Rights Movement, it addressed and spoke to the same issues. Cone gave "Black America," a theological doctrine that became the foundation of black-centered Christianity. It emphasized America's original sin of slavery, economic oppression, Jim Crow and lynching laws, systemic racism, and its eradication. So, these last words were spoken by the apostle Paul to his spiritual son Timothy: *"But know this, that in the last days perilous times will come: for men will be lovers of themselves, lovers of money, boasters, proud, blasphemers, disobedient to parents, unthankful, unholy, unloving, unforgiving, slanderers, without self-control, brutal, despisers of good, traitors, headstrong, haughty, lovers of pleasure rather than lovers of God, having a form of godliness but denying its power. And from such people turn away!"*

Setting the stage for the upcoming radical changes, transformation, and liberation of the church in the next few millennia. And no matter the violence and persecution that would befall the apostles and believers, it was all still under God's authority. The apostolic era of the Christian Church did not begin when Christ called the apostles, but after the crucifixion and up to the death of the apostle John. It started to make inroads after the Roman Empire sacked Jerusalem and liberated the church from the control of Jewish authority. This action by the Romans pushed the church out into the world and set it free to blossom into the church we see today. This turning point fulfilled and solidified two main character traits of Christianity that are still the central theme of its tenants today. To move outward to reach places where Christ's name has not been preached and to move inward to train hearts to learn more of Christ.[1]

---

1   Mark A. Noll. Turning Points Decisive Moments in the History of Christianity. (Grand Rapid, MI, Baker Academic, 2012), 1.

# CHAPTER 2

# AFRICA AND AFRICANS IN THE EARLY CHURCH
# MYTH OR FACT

*Psalm 68:31*

*Envoys will come out of Egypt;*

*Ethiopia will quickly*

*Stretch out her hands to God*

## Through the Eyes of An Enslaved Person

A terrible thing happened on our way to the cross. Fraud was perpetrated of satanic proportions. The victims of this fraud will not genuinely know the intent of this evil by its perpetrators other than the systemic domination and blinding power of Satan's kingdom on earth. However, there is clear and direct evidence of the benefits and privileges being enjoyed by the perpetrators who submit to this kingdom through oppression, poverty, depravity, humiliation, and indifference. There has always been an unspoken belief in America between the black and white societies that Christianity is a white man's religion. Many social black empowering movements throughout the history of America seem to subscribe to this doctrine. Which is based on two main themes:

- Oppression and continued oppression of black society

- Privilege status and position of white society socioeconomically, politically, environmentally, educationally, ecclesiastically, and legally.

The natural mind constantly struggles to reconcile the God of the Bible and the actual conditions and circumstances of suffering people and their experienced atrocities. The evil that happened was premeditatedly orchestrated with a false interpretation of scripture used to support and legitimize this satanic and evil way of living. It has produced a societal psychosis in the land that still exists today. The interpretation and legitimization were the idea or ideology that through all the atrocities perpetrated upon Black African society at the hands of White European society, ultimately, it was worth it, for in the end, through the white community, the black culture met Jesus Christ (but you still couldn't be set free). This psychosis still exists today in some as they believe that white society alone is responsible for the greatness of America and that our high standard of living in comparison to the rest of the world is because of the creativity, ingenuity, and intelligence of white society. This ethos has created an apostasy or falling away within the American church among both races. As stated, no one truly knows the personal motivations of individuals on why they would continue in this satanic fraud and participate in the propping up of it by such evil and depraved behavior, all the while professing "God Bless America." But what can be surmised and identified through intention and pre-meditated intention is that slavery was an economic gold mine for the young country and white society. Unofficially African Slavery began in America in 1619; I say unofficially because there is documented evidence that Africans were brought to the new world as early as the 1500s, and some say as early as the 1400s. But for this project, let us stay with the unofficial date of 1619 when the first Africans sailed up the "James River" on an English private ship captained by John Jope and dropped anchor in Jamestown, Virginia, where 20 to

30 Africans were led off and sold into a life of disgrace. As we take a closer look at this manufactured evil system, we see the humanics of our nature becoming much clearer.

In the history of the trans-Atlantic slave trade (1525-1866), twelve to thirteen million Africans were shipped to the New World. About ten million survived the dreaded Middle Passage, disembarking in North America, the Caribbean, and South America. About three to four hundred thousand were transported directly from Africa to North America. But this number is deceptive, and the reality is shocking to basic decency. The importation of enslaved people into the United States was banned by Congress (under Constitutional command) in 1808.

Yet, by 1860, the nation's black population had jumped from four hundred thousand to four and a half million, of which four million were slaves. The primary reason was because of a system called "**natural increase,**" a distinguishing feature of American-style slavery (these were the breeding farms where forced rapes were committed to hundreds of thousands of black women whose stories were never entirely told.) This is why, today in America, "The average African American today, according to Joanna Mountain at the genetics company 23andMe, "is 73.4 percent African, 24.1 percent European, and only 0.7 percent Native American" in their genetic makeup." The natural breeding of people was done to keep the economic engine running. This system is a level of evil that surpassed Nazi Germany or other recent human atrocities. In the U.S., on average, a slave mother gave birth to between nine and ten children, "twice as many as in the West Indies," according to the Gilder Institute of American History. Yet, in 1860, "less than ten percent of the slave population was over fifty and only three and a half percent was over 60." To ensure and solidify this evil empire, Virginia passed a series of laws so that this system would never end. Here are a few of those laws.

- 1662: "The General Assembly determined that Negro women's children serve according to the mother's condition."

- 1667: "The General Assembly passed "An act declaring the baptism of enslaved people does not exempt them from bondage. Because their baptism came from the piety and charity of their masters."

- 1669: "Virginia Passes an act regarding the casual killing of slaves: "If any slave resists his master (or other by his master's order correcting him) and by extremity of correction should chance to die, that his death should not be counted as a felony."

- 1670: "The General Assembly determined that know Negro nor Indians could buy Christian servants."

- 1672: The General Assembly passed "An act for the apprehension and suppression of runaways, Negroes and slaves," State gave authority to itself and any citizen to capture, wound, and or kill any runaway "slave for life" no matter where they are found.

- 1680: General Assembly passes "An act for preventing Negroes Insurrections": "Whereas the frequent meeting of considerable numbers of enslaved Negroes under the presence of feast and burials is judged dangerous. So, it shall not be lawful for any Negro or other enslaved person to carry or arm himself with any club, staff, gun, sword, or any other weapon of defense or offense, not go or depart from his master's grounds without a certificate from his master, and herby certificate not to granted except for particular and necessary operations. And every Negro caught not having a certificate will receive twenty lashes on his bare back well laid. Also, if any Negro is absent from his master's service and hides, lies, or is found lurking, it shall be lawful to kill said Negro."

So, we asked ourselves, where was the church when these atrocities transpired? The answer is not as simple as you may want it to be. Still, the cloaking and hiding behind religious piety and Christian charity through the so-called works of evangelism and conversion of an enslaved person were not of God, just another cover to prop up a satanic empire with unfathomable profit returns.

## Africans in the Bible

Because the truth is that African people did not need to meet Jesus through the brutality of Europeans because they knew him throughout scripture from the Old to New Testaments. How often do we turn a blind eye away from the promises that God has given to African people? Psalm 68:31 declares, *"Cush shall reach out its arms to God!"* (The early Church loved this promise, for they considered Cush a metaphor for the gentile Bride of Christ.) The Psalms predicted that one day, people would recognize the spirituality of the Cushites or Africans and declare that they had been born anew in Zion (87:3-6). Isaiah foretold that God would bring a remnant from Cush (11:11) and a redeemed people taking gifts to Zion (18:1-8). Zephaniah proclaimed that from beyond the rivers of Cush, God's people should bring offerings (3:10). Amos expresses God's concern for Cush: *"'Are you not like the Cushite's to me, O people of Israel?' says the Lord"* (9:7). Biblical scholars are aware that "Cush" sometimes refers to all of Africa, sometimes to all of Africa except Egypt, and sometimes to ancient Nubia, stretching from modern Aswan in the north to Khartoum in the south. Today most of this area lies in Sudan. But how can the general reader understand that Cush and Cushite (used 57 times in the Hebrew Bible) are a designation for an African nation and people? Because some versions of the Bible translate "Cush" as "Ethiopia," but this does not ordinarily designate the modern country of that name. David Adamo has suggested that the best translation is "Africa." As the upcoming map shows the region and its proximity to the biblical story, when one looks at the map, it's easy to see how Africa is a significant role player in the Bible story. We all have a right to know and applaud Africans' crucial Biblical role. People of African descent may claim the deep roots of their ancestors in the Bible. We read in Genesis that one of the rivers of Eden ran around the whole land of Cush, and another encircled the land of Havilah that yielded gold and onyx and bdellium (2:10-13). These products were found in antiquity, principally in the area now known as Sudan. If the Tigris and Euphrates rivers are located in Babylonia, then there is good reason to believe some of Eden lay in Africa. We are now told that the oldest human remains may also be traced to Africa. Hagar, the Egyptian concubine of

Abraham, may well have derived her ancestry from the south of Egypt. She, alone of all the Bible characters, gives God a name (Gen 16:13). Like Abraham, she meets God in the form of an angel. She is promised that her progeny shall become a great nation (Gen 21:18). Moses' Cushite wife aroused the bitter jealousy of his sister Miriam. (Num 12:11-16). Amusingly, Miriam, who resents her black sister-in-law, becomes white with leprosy until she mends her ways. If this Cushite wife was Zipporah, then Moses' father-in-law is Jethro, the priest, who instituted the judicial, administrative, and sacrificial patterns of Israel (Ex 18:1-27). He and his family had received the exiled Moses during Moses' forty years as a shepherd in Sinai.

Zipporah had understood the importance of circumcision and performed the ritual on their sons (Ex 18:1-27). Even if the Cushite wife refers to a second spouse, then Moses also looks to his new father-in-law for guidance and direction (Num. 10:29-32; Jdg. 1:16). When the Israelites settled in the land of

Canaan, there were Africans among them. Some may have left Egypt along with the Israelites at the time of the Exodus; others came with military invaders (1 Kg 14:25-28; 2 Chr 12:2-3; 14:9-15; cf. 16:8). An Ethiopian colony was created at Gerar as a buffer between Egypt and Judah. Thus, the Ethiopians became permanent residents in Palestine, remaining there until Hezekiah (715-685 BCE). Accordingly, we read, "*They journeyed to the entrance of Gedor, to the east side of the valley, to seek pasture for their flocks, where they found rich, good pasture, and the land was vast, quiet, and peaceful; for the former inhabitants there belonged to Ham*" (1 Chr 4:39-40). Further, a group of Philistines and Arabs was said to be settled "*near the Ethiopians*" (2 Chr 21:16).

Persons of African descent appear to have taken an active role in Israel's social and political life. The bride in Song of Solomon is "black and beautiful" (Song 1:5). A Cushite who possessed tact, discretion, and a high position in the royal court appeared as a trusted courtier sent to tell David news of Absalom's death (2

Sam 18:19-32). Africans continued to enjoy royal favor, as Solomon married an Egyptian princess (1 Kg 9:16, 24; 2 Chr. 8:11) and received the Queen of Sheba (1 Kg 10:1-13; 2 Chr. 9:1-2). This influential queen ruled dark-skinned peoples on both sides of the Red Sea, and she may well have initially come to Solomon to negotiate a trade treaty with his growing maritime power. Though she tested him with hard questions, in the end, she told him all that was in her heart. It appears that Solomon found a kindred spirit in this black woman with whom he could discourse freely. Whether or not that relationship was sexual, there is evidence that other alliances produced children. Zephaniah, a descendant of Hezekiah, is called the son of Cushi and brings remarkable prophecies about Cush (Zeph 1:1; 3:10). Jehudi, the courtier sent to bear Jeremiah's message from Baruch to King Zedekiah, appears to have had a Cushite ancestor (Jer 36:14). Faithfully, Baruch stands before the king, reading the words of God.

In contrast, the king slashes the scroll and casts it

into the fire (Jer 36: 21, 23). Ebed-Melek, a confidential advisor of the king, is identified as a Cushite four times (Jer 38:7, 10, 12; 39:16). Believing that Jeremiah was bringing God's authentic voice to Judah, Ebed-Melek risked his life to rescue the prophet from the cistern and secure for him a hearing with the king. Jeremiah commends the courtier's faith (39:15-18) and proclaims a special covenant of God's protection to him.

When Cushite pharaohs ruled over Egypt, they contracted military alliances with Israel and Judah, especially during the Twenty-fifth Cushite Dynasty. Sabacho (716-701 BC, called so in 2 Kings 17:4) acquired a coalition against Assyria with Hoshea, king of Israel, while Tirhakah (690-664) came to the aid of Hezekiah when Jerusalem was besieged (2 Kg 19:9; Is 37:9). Mortuary figurines of Tirhakah reveal his African features, and his enormous statue still towers above the great temple complex at Karnak.[2]

---

2    Priscilla Papers Academic Journal. Winter 2000. Scripture and Race

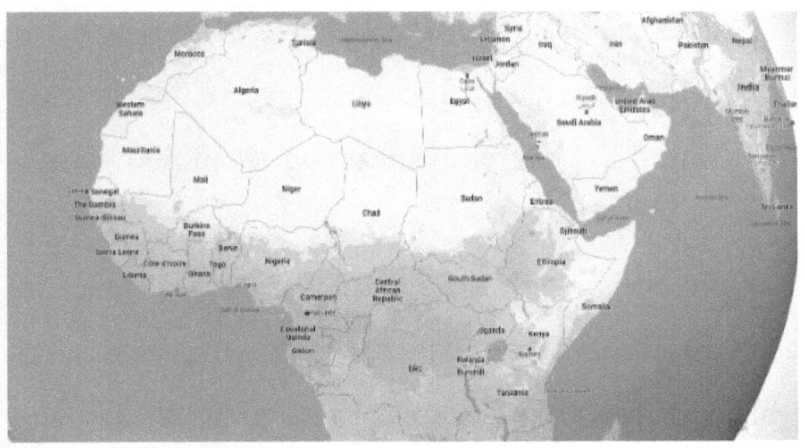

## African Bishops in the Early Church

In the early period of the sub-apostolic era, African Bishops played a prominent role in defending, spreading, and teaching the Christian faith. Men like:

Clement of Alexandria (150-215) was a Christian philosopher keen to win pagan intellectuals to Christ. He directed a catechetical school at Alexandria and wrote important exhortations to the heathen and Christians, calling them to a perfect life in Christ.

Another African, Origen (185-254), became the director of a catechetical school at age 18. His was the finest mind the church would produce in 300 years.

Origen was highly successful in debating Jews, pagans, and Gnostics and is credited with destroying Gnosticism. This essential biblical scholar, theologian, exegete, and pioneer in biblical criticism produced the Hexapla, comparing six versions of the Bible. He profoundly influenced the theological thought of the succeeding centuries.

Tertullian (160-225) was a pagan lawyer who converted to Christianity. He authored apologetic, theological, and controversial works and was the first theologian to write in Latin. He formulated the doctrine of the Trinity and coined nearly a thousand new words to explain Christian truths.

Athanasius (296-373) was the Bishop of Alexandria and a significant theologian and writer. He was the chief upholder of the doctrine that Christ was both man and God and was the principal opponent of the Arian doctrine that Jesus was a man rather than God. Even as a very young deacon, he was influential at the Council of Nicaea. Opponents referred to him as the "black dwarf." He was repeatedly exiled and persecuted, but his principles ultimately prevailed at the Council of Constantinople in 381.

Cyril, who died in 444, was also the Bishop of Alexandria. He brilliantly represented and systematized the teachings of Athanasius and other Alexandrians. He was a vigorous opponent of heresy.

Perpetua and Felicitas were two martyrs who died in the Carthage arena in 202. Their story was widely used in winning others to Christ.

Cyprian, Bishop of Carthage, died a martyr in 258. He possessed a profound knowledge of the Scriptures, wrote critical theological works, fought heresy, and insisted on the unity of the Church.

Lactantius (c. AD 317) is best known for his Institutes, described as the "most comprehensive apology which Christianity created before the end of the time of persecution." The central theme of the Institutes is justice. Lactantius insisted that God had given humanity a way of life open to all people regardless of race, education, sex, color, or creed.

St. Maurice of Aganum (born about 287) was a Roman general who refused to kill Christians during the slave revolt in Gaul. He declared to the emperor Maximian: We cannot obey you without denying God, the Creator of all things, our Master as well as yours, whether you acknowledge it or not. He was slaughtered by imperial decree along with his regiment for his defense of enslaved people.

G. Marius Victorinus (280-363) was a Neoplatonist professor of rhetoric with a brilliant record as a philosopher and scholar. Educated in Africa but taught in Rome, he wrote theological and devotional works that led to Augustine's conversion.

Augustine (354-430), Bishop of Hippo, was one of the Doctors of the Church. A profoundly influential theologian, he dealt with three heresies: Manichaeism, Donatism, and Pelagianism. Augustine had remarkable insights into the human heart and soul. His most famous work is Confessions, written to describe his conversion and win others to Christ by detailing the philosophical basis for Christianity.

Monica (331-387) was Augustine's prayerful and powerful mother. And many more that I have not mentioned in this book.

## Africa and the Nicaea Council

Africans were not only an instrumental and entangled part of ancient biblical life, but they were also part of saving and preserving the Christian faith we practice today as Emperor Constantine emerged victorious from his Roman civil wars to capture the emperor's seat. Constantine believed that his victory was preordained by God and wanted to bring Christianity into mainstream Roman life and ultimately become the empire's official religion. The Nicaea Council, the very first of its kind, was crucial to the emperor's vision for Christianity and Rome. An ecumenical call to eighteen hundred bishops throughout the Roman Empire to debate and resolve an arising issue within the Church of Alexandria. This church is one of the original Apostolic Sees of Christianity alongside Rome, Antioch, Constantinople, and Jerusalem. (The church at Alexandria is said to be founded by the Apostle John-Mark). The issue within the church was a disagreement over the nature of

Jesus in his relationship with the Father. In particular, whether he, Jesus, was begotten by the Father from his being, meaning he also has no beginning, or was he created by the Father and has a start. The latter would relegate him to prophet status and no longer divinity. Led by African bishop St. Alexander and Athanasius, of the estimated 300 bishops, only two voted for the latter position. Those two were banished along with Arius, the founder of Arianism, to Illyria. The council also agreed on when to celebrate "Easter," the essential feast of the ecclesiastical calendar.

# CHAPTER 3

# A DIVIDED CHURCH

*Matthew 12:25*

*But Jesus knew their thoughts and said to them:*
*"Every kingdom divided against itself is brought to*
*desolation, and every city or house divided against*
*itself will not stand."*

## Divide By Doctrine

U ltimately, Nicaea brought about the first split in the Christian church over doctrine. The heretic presbyter Arius and his Arianism doctrine began to spread a heretical theology that held to the belief that Christ was not divine, but a created being in the church of Alexandria in Egypt. This doctrine was fervently opposed in a jointly agreed-upon statement by all the bishops in attendance except for three. The information is called the "Nicaean Creed."

*"We believe in one God, the Father Almighty, Maker of all things visible and invisible. And in one Lord Jesus Christ, the Son of God, begotten of the Father the only-begotten; that is, of the essence of the Father, God of God, Light of Light, very God of very God, begotten, not made, being of one substance with the Father; by whom all things were made both in heaven and on earth; who for us men, and our salvation, came down and was incarnate and was made man; he suffered, and the third day he rose again,*

*ascended into heaven; from thence he shall come to judge the quick and the dead. And in the Holy Ghost. But those who say: 'There was a time when he was not,' and 'He was not before he was made,' and 'He was made out of nothing,' or 'He is of another substance' or 'essence,' or 'The Son of God is created,' or 'changeable,' or 'alterable'—they are condemned by the holy catholic and apostolic Church."*

This creed was primarily accepted by all denominations of the Christian church in some form or another, with slight abbreviations made over the centuries depending on the denomination. That is, until the "Great Schism."

## The Great Schism

A split of the universal church took place in 1054 AD over a doctrinal issue called the "Filioque Clause" in the Nicene Creed, and this became known as the great schism. A Latin phrase translation and addition of "And" to the phrase "the Son" now read "And the Son" was accepted by the Western Church while opposed by the Eastern Church. The First Council of Constantinople confirmed the Nicene Creed in 381: *"We believe in the Holy Spirit, the Lord, the giver of life, who proceeds from the Father. Who with the Father and the Son is worshiped and glorified."* And then with the filioque in 589. *"We believe in the Holy Spirit, the Lord, the giver of life, who proceeds from the Father and the Son. Who with the Father and the Son is worshiped and glorified."*

This subtle dispute concerns the person in the Godhead and the nature of the Trinity. It became a source of friction between the east and west, most likely over who had the authority to make and approve this change. This, along with rising Papal authority, became more than the unity could support, and the split happened.

The next big split came in the early fifteenth century in the "Protestant Reformation" or Martin Luther's Protests. This split occurred over the Roman Catholic Church practice called "Indulgences." Bishops of the church granted forgiveness of sins to the aristocracy and anyone who could afford it. Luther argued that the

Pope had no authority over purgatory and based the reformation on the theological doctrine of justification by faith and not of works. As the church moved to the new world, we saw it split again, this time by race.

## Divided by Race

Before the United States of America became a country, the churches were already divided along racial lines. In 1449 Spain and the Catholic Church doctrine/ concept of "Purity of Blood" was introduced to the old world and exploded in the New World. It focused more on ancestry than religion. It was the child of an earlier church doctrine called **"Limpieza de Sangre"** or **"Cleanliness of Blood"** (If this term sounds familiar, it should because it was Adolf Hitler's mission statement for the creation of the "Third Reich "and the Aryan master race). In 1455 it was blessed by Pope Nicolas V when he signed the "Papal Bull of 1455," which justified keeping Jewish and Muslim converts out of Christianity and the expansion of (black) African slavery within early

Iberian (Spain) colonies and the acquisition of more African captives and territory. Still, the same decree also provided a legal framework for sub-Saharan Africans to negotiate with Iberian/Spanish authorities on equal footing and to make claims of Black Africans. Most historians regard this Papal document as the beginning of the trans-Atlantic slave trade.

This ultimately led to the institution of chattel slavery, which was prevalent in the New World from the inception of America and was well-established with other people even before colonization. With the New World colonists, it grew into an official institution with taxes, property rights, insurance claims, and the like after the country's founding in 1776.

In the 1780s, an enslaved person named Andrew Bryan preached to a small group of enslaved people in Savannah, Ga. White citizens had Bryan arrested and whipped. Despite persecution and harassment, the church grew, and by 1790 it became the First African Church of Savannah. By 1816, the first independent black denomination, the African Methodist Episcopal Church, came into existence and was quickly followed by the African Methodist Episcopal Zion Church in 1821. This forced division of racial segregation in the church house due to racial hatred, white supremacist behaviors, and Satan's schemes to divide a people, nation, and God's kingdom. It quickly became a self-imposed way of life and worship that persists today.

This deep-rooted blight on the American heart and consciousness has caused significant damage to societies by affecting its citizens individually and collectively, increasing racism and separatism through self-imposed segregation outside the church.[3] The American culture has been forced to incorporate legal terms like inclusivity, diversity, integration, and desegregation into our offices, neighborhoods, and organizations, for-profits or non-profits, all to penetrate and remove the stain of our country's original immoral and evil sin from our hearts,

---

3   Vischer, Robert K. (2001). "Racial Segregation in American Churches and Its Implications for School Vouchers". *Florida Law Review*. 53: 193.

psyche, and consciousness. It shows that we tend to gravitate back to what is comfortable if left up to us. Our natural desire to be with others who look like us creates a self-fulfilling prophecy of shared life experiences that we call culture.

Our Human culture has a sickness, which is "sin." Sin has many symptoms, like prejudice and racism, which divide and continue to divide people. The question that must be asked is, "What is the kingdom of God and its culture in the daily life of the people of the world look like"? From his miraculous birth, Jesus was sent to destroy the works and schemes of the devil, not to submit to them[4]. No sick person brought to Jesus was ever told to accept the sickness because it was God's will. The ministry of Jesus was an onslaught upon the works of Satan, whether his works were manifested in disorder, demon possession among the people, or hypocrisy, cruelty, and hardheartedness among the rulers.[5]

---

4   Winter D. Ralph, Hawthorne C. Steven. Perspective on the Worlds Christian Movement. (Pasadena Ca, William Carey Library, 2009). 99.

5   Ibid.

## Divide By Status

The Epistle of James admonishes the Christians who follow Christ to remove partiality/bias from their hearts, for there is no place for bias in God's kingdom. James 2:1 *"My brethren, do not hold the faith of our Lord Jesus Christ, the Lord of glory, with partiality. For if there should come into your assembly, a man with gold rings, in fine apparel, and a poor man in filthy clothes should also come into your assembly. You pay attention to the one wearing the fine clothes and say to him, "You sit here in a good place," and say to the poor man, "You stand there," or, "Sit here at my footstool," have you not shown partiality among yourselves, and become judges with evil thoughts?"*

Here we see God's view of bias and indifference starting in the heart and then manifesting into judging behavior motivated by evil or ill-willed thoughts towards others who are deemed as unworthy, less than, inferior, or not of an acceptable status, ultimately dispersing caste and stigma upon a group regulating them into lives of hardship and exclusion. Bias is one of Satan's oldest and simplest schemes designed for the maximum effect of dividing people by race, status, and gender. It can be the root cause of envy, jealousy, resentment, and hatred.

Another reason God speaks against discriminatory behavior among the saints is that it violates the "Great Command and Commission," which asked us to love him and our neighbors likewise, as well as go to all people and present him and this gospel message to them throughout the world. Bias also produces a tolerance within us to accept and justify our prejudices.

# Chapter 4

# GOD'S KINGDOM MAN'S WORLD

*Matthew 10:34*

*"Do not think that I came to bring peace on earth.*
*I did not come to bring peace but a sword."*

## Breaking Into

The brutal crucifixion of Christ did several things to change the course of the world's cultural and spiritual trajectories. The Bible describes it this way: at the time of Christ's death, the curtain in the temple was ripped from the top down, darkness covered the area for three hours during the day, and graves opened. These events represent a violent spiritual entrance into the physical world by the Holy Spirit, who was sent to empower and embody his church so that it may confront sin wherever it is. The birth of Christ also produced violent outcomes and consequences as King Herod slaughtered hundreds of innocent babies in a jealous effort to stop Christ's works of healing and deliverance.

So as Christ worked, so must the church; God's breaking into human history challenged the powers that oppressed and dehumanized, unmasking the pretensions and intentions of principalities and strengths along with their manifesto of spiritual wickedness.[6] Because Satan, through sin, had so grievously blinded, divided, and oppressed the children of God, the "Cross" is the symbol of the coming kingdom in the father's hands on the other side of the grave. The church has been empowered to show a sin-filled dying world within its constraints and limitations in its present age, the reality of God's kingdom to come. This theology may have to establish itself in many methodologies, from dogma, grace, charity, love, and compassion even to the iron will resistance in defensive forms but yet unwilling to bow, bend or accept the oppression and dehumanization of others as a natural way of existence.

## God's War Plan

The ancient Hebrew people, like most people, based their national identity on their relationship with Yahweh and his ongoing presence in their lives. If their enemies were defeated and had a good harvest and sufficient

---

6    Ibid.

rainfall, their relationship was solid, and God was present. So, whenever they went into captivity, they suffered an identity crisis with weak and wondering faith as to the reality of the divine and his power to provide and protect them and their interest. This psychology is standard among humans, even in today's societies. The land is well-filled with milk and honey, fruits, vegetation, fresh water, rich wildlife, trees, plants, and flowers (God Bless America). But let the drought, wildfires, floods, and destructive weather come, and faith becomes weak and wandering. Placing trust in God for material blessings, ease and comfort living, problem-free lives, good paying jobs with corner offices, or now post-pandemic (Full Remote Work Schedules) is placing your faith into the hands of evil and volatile powers and principalities who now have access to your heart, hopes, and dreams. God's war plan is to liberate you so you can take back your power.

In ancient times with the Hebrew people, the narrative and conversation had to be flipped from God abandoning his people out of fear and impotence to the people leaving God for desired sin. Once this was the reality, the fight back to God began through repentance. An example of these dynamics can be seen in one-sided relationships, where selfishness dominates, and boundaries are violated. If not corrected, it can escalate into intimate partner violence emotionally, psychologically, and physically because of misperceived perceptions by the abuser. But in God's war plan, we are never cut off or denied access; if we have breath, we can repent and begin to take our power back from the world's dictates of oppressive, dehumanizing schemes that cause us to perpetuate evil on one another.

## A Loss Gets Us Lost on the Battlefield

How did we get so lost, and why can't we find our way out of this national and international disgrace? What keeps blinding us from the truth? Why are greed, hate, resentment, and hardheartedness our immediate responses to the issues of life? Who can deliver us from this wretchedness? God can, for he has a war plan, the ultimate "Hidden War" fought within the human consciousness, where the forces of good meet the forces of evil. Evil's allies are greed, racism/bias, division, and indifference wrapped up in the human sickness of sin. This is the worldview where Satan's kingdom reigns and its mission is to oppress and dehumanize the human spirit, crush our hopes, and stifle our dreams—rendering the human into a shell of their potential. It has been said that African American history is not slavery, but instead, African American history was interrupted *by* slavery. For five hundred years, the world has given in to its natural sinful desires and manifested the worst of our behavior. We have lived in this ideological dysfunctionality for so long that it has changed humanity for the worst. Our evil is always present with us and, in most cases, dominates our perspectives. As long as we as a society continue to value Satan's materialistic world over God's eternal one, we will continue to live in states of covertness, comparing, competing, envying, measuring, blaming, lusting, and hating one another.

We are incapable of separating our losses and denials from anger and disappointment. What is dangerously sad is that this attitude is built upon a core set of spiritual beliefs that American sociologist Christian Smith Ph.D. from the University of Notre Dame, in his book "Soul Searching: The Religious and Spiritual Lives of Americans," defines as MTD (Moralistic Therapeutic Deism). Even though smith focused his research and study on Christian youth, I believe it encompasses western religious belief systems in America. MTD is defined this way:

- A belief that God created the universe and watched over it.

- God also wants people to be good and fair in their treatment and dealings with others, as the Bible teaches.

- God wants you to live a happy life.

- God loves you, never chastises you, and is only involved in your life when you have a problem to be fixed.

- Good people go to heaven.

This type of American Christianity makes up a significant part of American society and is a moral betterment program if you follow the script through behavior. The danger here is that it has very little to do with the gospel of Jesus Christ and runs counter to biblical teachings on being a good person.

Romans 3: 23-26 *"For all have sinned and fall short of the glory of God, being justified freely by His grace through the redemption that is in Christ Jesus whom God set forth as a propitiation by His blood, through faith, to demonstrate His righteousness, because in His forbearance God had passed over the sins that were previously committed, to demonstrate at present His righteousness, that He might be just and the justifier of the one who has faith in Jesus.*" This passage explains our desperate need for a savior, for even being good is too hard for humans according to God's righteous standard.

Matthew 19: 16-22 "*Now behold, one came and said to Him, 'Good Teacher, what good thing shall I do that I may have eternal life?*" So He said to him, '*Why do you call me good? No one is good but one, and that is God. But if you want to enter into life, keep the commandments.*" He said to Him, '*Which ones?' Jesus said, 'You shall not murder, you shall not commit adultery, you shall not steal, you shall not bear false witness, honor your father and your mother, and you shall love your neighbor as yourself.' The young man said to Him, 'All these things I have kept from my youth. What do I still lack?' Jesus said to him, 'If you want to be perfect, go, sell what you have and give to the poor, and you will have treasure in heaven; and come, follow me.*" But when the young man heard that saying, he went away sorrowful, for he had great possessions.

In this passage, we read what Jesus says: no one is good but his father. But more importantly, is the requestor's attitude "what must I do to inherit eternal life" in other words, what must I perform to have this? It is all about us and never about Christ and how he can change us. The next thing was his elevation to God-like status when he professed to have kept all the commandments, more pride, just like his first statement. Then came his despair and discouragement when the reality of the standard confronted him. Sell all that you have and follow me. This seems to sum up the mission statement of American Christianity, two altars of pride and despair. Pride in the performing and presentation of God's blessings through health and wealth and the sadness when the reality of life comes to meet God saving faith in our lives and finds it absent. Here is where health and wealth loss can get you lost even more.

## The Ordained Church

Jesus said to his disciples in Matthew 16:18, "*And I*

*also say to you that you are Peter, and on this rock, I will build my church, and the gates of Hades shall not prevail against it."* This church, the ecclesia or called out ones, we who have been called out of the world through faith in him. We have repented and recognized our lostness and our need for a savior. This church is called to preach Christ crucified as the apostle Paul instructs. We are not here to promote self as an example and blueprint for salvation but to always point all towards Christ and his excellent cross.

Satan desires that we never meet the crucified Christ and remain ignorant and selfish in our beliefs. We present a self-help gospel cloaked in superficial good works, meaning works that can be seen by men and feed our egos. So, as stated at the beginning of this chapter, "God's War" plan is to shock us out of our blessed ignorance, which is insulated by fantasy, ego, and lies, into the reality of our sinfulness which has been manifested into a trail of misery that we have perpetrated on each other for greed's sake, for significance's sake, for ego's sake, for hate's sake. The work of the ecclesia is to penetrate this thick wall of deception in us so we can be set free. As a pastoral counselor and chaplain with over twenty-five hundred hours of counseling sessions in America and Johannesburg, South Africa, my methodology is "Solution Focus Pastoral Counseling," which is founded on God's war plan found in Isaiah 61: 1-3:

*"The Spirit of the Lord God is upon Me Because the Lord has anointed Me To preach good tidings to the poor; He has sent Me to heal the brokenhearted, to proclaim liberty to the captives, And the opening of the prison to those who are bound; To proclaim the acceptable year of the Lord, and the day of vengeance of our God; to comfort all who mourn. To console those who mourn in Zion, to give them beauty for ashes, The oil of joy for mourning, The garment of praise for the spirit of heaviness; That they may be called trees of righteousness, The planting of the Lord, that He may be glorified."*

Even though I call it God's war plan, it's his love plan because John 3:16 says, *"For God so loved the world that He gave his only begotten son, that whoever believes in him should not perish but have everlasting life."*

# Chapter 5

# POLITICS AND THE CHURCH

*Matthew 22:21*

*They said to Him, "Caesar's." And He said to them,*
*"Render therefore to Caesar the things that are Caesar's,*
*and to God the things that are God's."*

## Separation of Church and State

The United States of America's foundation document, the US Constitution, is the document that governs the lives of every American citizen, resident alien, visitor, and the like. It comprises twenty-seven ratified amendments, with the first ten adopted by the Continental Congress through a series of hard-fought debates, fights, and compromises between the thirteen states. The very first amendment of the "Bill of Rights" says, "Congress shall make no law respecting an establishment of religion or prohibiting the free exercise thereof. It is classified as an "establishment clause" It means that people in public authority, like elected officials, judges, teachers, and principals cannot promote religion or have assemblies to promote one religion over another including atheism.

The US Constitution has an older sister document that is not legally binding but is the heart and soul of America, and that is the "Declaration of Independence" that starts like this "We hold these truths to be self-evident, that all men are created equal, that their creator endows them with certain unalienable rights, that among these are life, liberty and the pursuit of happiness." This document is the pronouncement from the thirteen colonies on why they went to war to resist the Kingdom of Great Britain. It is the heart and soul of white American society's belief system. But it is *not* so for African or other non-white immigrants. The irony here is that the same new world church that advocated resistance against England and its religious persecution of the protestant faith was not so eager to support the Africans a few years later in the formulation of the legally binding US Constitution **(Here is where Christ asked us to give Caesar our loyalty, our professionalism but give God our sinful hearts through repentance)**. Some would argue that due to the privilege and benefits of slavery, these founding fathers and leaders enjoyed most being enslavers and partakers in the benefits of free labor, legal rape, murder, and unbridled torture. That produced wealth and riches desperately needed for the upstart new country; they never gave God their repentant hearts.

## Three-Fifths Compromise

There is no evidence more blatant and damning to the hypocrisy of the "Declaration of Independence" as the three-fifth clause in the constitution. In a nutshell, the three-fifths compromise provided southern states of the original thirteen colonies the legal right to claim up to sixty percent of their enslaved population towards congressional representation, which naturally increased these states' seats. Why was this introduced? During the formulation of the constitution, there was much mistrust amongst the delegates from the original colonies.

It took sixty votes among them before they could begrudgingly agree on the Bill of Rights. Because of their fear of an all-powerful and tyrannical federal government that would have the power to usurp their freedoms and finances or larger states getting precedents over the smaller ones, they came up with a legal way to use the enslaved for the greater good of preserving unity within the newly formed national government. They gave them three-fifths of personhood status and zero representation. This was so well received that it was the only clause that could not be amended for twenty years from 1788 to 1808.

Here we see the church actively missing opportunities to present the teachings of the bible and Jesus Christ because of the pursuit of their greed and lust. This ideology is still being fought by today's generations of Americans but not only from a racial perspective but also power and positioning. Today we see many African American politicians coming out of the black church or willing to use a willing black church to establish a political power base. Organizations like the "Southern Christian Leadership Conference" of the 1950s and '60s came out of the Ebenezer Baptist Church in Atlanta, Georgia, and were led by clergy and lawyers.

Today one of our current US Senators is the senior pastor of that church. Then you have non-profit Christian organizations like the National Action Network, founded as an advocate for civil rights organization and has transformed itself into a power broker lobbying group. These are just a few Christian organizations present as Christ-like but have a duality of purpose. And have taken root in African American and poor communities with a desire to keep people in dependency circumstances so they can continue to be part of the power base that mainly serves leadership. In America, there is much profit in helping the poor, especially with public funding. Independent Christian Churches and ministries, whether they be black or white, that raise their own money and labor to produce food pantries, soup kitchens, clothing drives, housing, and school programs, find themselves in never-ending uphill battles with politicians who view them as threats to their base and in many cases work against these groups to wear out their volunteer spirit and exhaust their funding. This dynamic is like the three-fifths compromise in that poor people are manipulated and used to fulfill and maintain leaders and their lifestyles, but now it is done by people who look like them.

Earlier in the book, we discussed the difference between the American management of enslaved people versus the West Indies, and the only difference that seems to separate America from the rest of the slave trading nations is this methodology called "natural increase," where more enslaved women were brought into the country so breeding farms could be established. But the real and only motivation for these methods, along with Federal legal support, was money and lots of it. At its height, enslaved people generated annually three billion dollars for the US economy. In today's dollars, adjusting for inflation, this works out to fifty-four and half billion dollars. Greed for large profits was much greater than the little moral outrage that a few Christian organizations, such as the Quakers, abolitionists, and Wilberforce society, could muster initially.

This was ultimately revealed as the thought processes through the US. Supreme Court's decision in the 1857 **"Dred Scott Vs. Sandford" where the court said this**

**about enslaved Africans "they had no rights which the white man was bound to respect."** This decision was codified and solidified after the fact of "chattel slavery" in America. The importation of enslaved African people halted due to the British parliament's passage of the 1807 slave trade act. So, the American enslavers created breeding farms to produce more workers. The function of such breeding farms was to have as many enslaved people as possible for sale and distribution throughout the South to meet its needs. The locations of the two largest breeding farms were in Richmond, VA, and the Maryland Eastern Shore. What made this abomination of breeding enslaved people an acceptable practice? Laws and practices that transformed the view of enslaved people from «personhood» into «thinghood" became normalized. This way, enslaved people could be bought and sold as chattels without challenging society›s religious beliefs and social norms. All rights were to the owner of the enslaved person, with the enslaved person having no rights of self-determination either to their person, spouse, or children.

The Holy Scriptures were even misinterpreted to
support this abomination by using Genesis 9 as Ham,
the son of Noah and the father of the Hamite race
and originator of the Hamitic bloodline, which is the
bloodline of the people of central and sub-Sahara
regions of Africa. And because God cursed Ham, so was
his bloodline. This now-defunct model of dividing the
human race established by Europeans to undergird and
prop up colonialism and slavery throughout the world
was used in America to legally and morally justify this
abomination. It dealt with this region of Africa, below
Egypt, from the red sea to the continent's east coast.

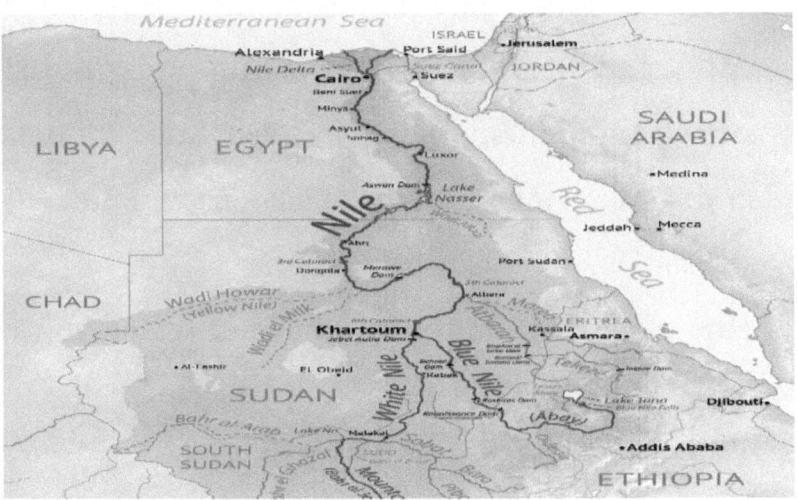

## The Trauma of Natural Increase

As the political battle to reinstitute Roe Vs. Wade ramps up, women all over America and around the world watch closely. But let us not forget that this decision of control and enslavement is not new thinking to our land. As a professional counselor, chaplain, and pastor, I have had my fair share of counseling sessions with sexual abuse victims. This act of extreme violence perpetrated upon the person of women and girls leaves many with more lifelong emotional and spiritual trauma than physical ones. We now know through research and studies that sexual abuse victims can experience these physical conditions (Chronic pelvic pain, premenstrual syndrome, gastrointestinal disorders, and various chronic pain disorders, including headache, back pain, and facial pain).[7]

The psychological consequences of sexual abuse are immediate; they are (shock, disbelief, denial, fear,

---

7    Tim Clinton, Ron Hawkins. The Quick Reference Guide to Biblical Counseling
     Personal and Emotional issues, Baker Books, 2009. Pg. 221,222

confusion, anxiety, and withdrawal. They may also suffer from emotional detachment, sleep disturbance, and flashbacks. They also can experience guilt, nervousness, phobias, substance abuse, depression, alienation, sexual dysfunction, and suicidal behavior).[8] One can only imagine the suffering of enslaved African women who also bore the suffering from the trauma of Infanticide; as the late Toni Morrison described in her book "Beloved," no statistical data exist showing the percentage of enslaved African women who killed their children freeing them from a life of bondage. Still, we can safely assume that it did happen often. The trauma did not stop here but has become intergenerational by creating a self-fulfilling prophecy that has emotionally, spiritually, and psychologically enslaved both white and black generations. We see it in the ethos of daily cultural life manifested through class, caste, privilege, disparities, and perspectives. It touches all aspects of

---

8    Tim Clinton, Ron Hawkins. The Quick Reference Guide to Biblical Counseling Personal and Emotional issues, Baker Books, 2009. Pg. 222

American and global life through poverty, physical and mental health, crime and incarceration, life expectancy, and infant mortality. It seems to answer the question posed by James Baldwin in his book "Go Tell it on the Mountain."

Could a curse come down so many ages? Has the American experiment been doomed from the start because of slavery? Are we, as a society, constantly trying to turn away from our shame through the distractions of wealth and pleasure? Can true repentance save us? Can we forgive one another for the past deeds of our ancestors? We must if we want to break this curse.

# CHAPTER 6

# THE UNITED STATES SUPREME COURT

*Romans 10: 11-13*

*The Scripture says, "Everyone who believes in him will not be put to shame." For there is no distinction between Jew and Greek; for the same Lord is Lord of all, bestowing his riches on all who call on him. "everyone who calls on the name of the Lord will be saved."*

## Court's Early Attitude towards Enslaved Africans

To say that the court's decisions were completely biased toward enslaved Africans is not entirely accurate. The court shows consistency in not interfering or overturning many states' supreme court decisions in northern states but also held up the law of the southern states as well as vigorously enforced the "Fugitive slave law of 1850," which was part of the US congress compromise of 1850 to the Southern slave-owning states. Here is a list of a few of the hundreds of cases filed by Africans on their behalf to obtain their freedoms throughout the country.

- 1779 Brakke V. Lovell in the Vermont Superior Court decided in favor of Pompey Brakke. Brakke was held as an enslaved person by Elijah Lovell after slavery was made illegal in Vermont. Lovell failed to appear, and Brakkee was awarded four hundred pounds sterling.

- 1781 Brom and Bett V. Ashley in the Berkshire County Court of Common Pleas: Slave Elizabeth Freeman, also known as Bet, Mum Bet, or MumBet, was freed on the basis that the Massachusetts constitution provided that "all men are born free and equal" This case was the precedent case.

- 1783 Commonwealth V. Jennison in Massachusetts Supreme Judicial Court: Justice William Cushing instructs a Jury that "slavery is in my judgment as effectively abolished as it can be by granting rights and privileges wholly incompatible and repugnant to its existence."

- 1830 North Carolina V. Mann in the Supreme Court of North Carolina: The court ruled that slave-owners had absolute authority over their slaves in the territory before Indiana's state constitution ban on slavery.

- 1834 North Carolina V. Negro Will in the Supreme Court of North Carolina: Judge William Gaston held that enslaved people who killed their owner or overseer in self-defense could not be found guilty of murder but manslaughter at most.

- 1838 Hinds V. Brazealle in the Supreme Court of Mississippi: denied a deed of manumission in Ohio for a citizen of a Mississippi mixed-race son and his slave mother because it was against Mississippi's statutes. This deed needed an act by the state legislature. Otherwise, it was considered fraudulent.

- 1841 United States V. Libellants and Claimants of the Schooner Amistad in the Supreme Court of the United States: The Court ruled, "As Africans in question were never legal property, they were not criminals and had rightfully defended themselves in mutiny. They were unlawfully kidnapped, and the court directed the President to transport them to Africa."

- 1857 Dred Scott V. Sandford in the United States Supreme Court. The court ruled that "people of African descent imported into the United States and held as enslaved people, or their decedents, whether or not they were enslaved, were not included under the Constitution and could not be citizens of the United States."

As you have read, the issue of slavery in America depended upon what part of the country you lived in.

## Case Studies: Daily Life of the Enslaved

As I am not a constitutional lawyer or a lawyer of any kind, I cannot present legal case studies on the legal merits of each case. But what can be discussed is the fact that these cases exist and what that meant to daily life for the Africans in America. There has always been a segment of white American society; maybe a portion of this segment are Christian believers with hearts that dictate speech and behavior, revealing that they favor true democracy but still desire power to control a minority base. The fact that some of these cases ended up in victories for enslaved Africans is only a testament to their commitment to pursuing freedom and all their allies who saw the fights through to the end.

But it reveals another side of life in America for the enslaved people of this land, an ethos that persists today. The African American community has been described as "aggressive, sensitive, and complainers," but these descriptions do not just identify a people, but a cultural experience suffered through for generations. Currently, there has been a trend of incidents where law-abiding white citizens have called the police on law-abiding black citizens who have been in areas and or neighborhoods where the white person feels uncomfortable by the black person's presence and demands that the black citizen show identification or justify why they are in the area or neighborhoods. This is no different from these cases where African enslaved people must prove and fight for their legitimacy and legality to exist even when they are supposed to be free. Videos on social media are tagged with the phrase "driving while black" to shed light on this ongoing issue while people are being stopped and questioned merely because they are black.

Behind the legal drama in the courtroom was an authentic societal atmosphere that believed the African enslaved people were not worthy of equality and fairness and were not recognized as simply human beings. Living life under the threat that your life could change for the worse at any moment, depending on which white person you encounter, produces a next-level type of community psychosis and emotional suffering, having anxiety, stress, nervousness, paralysis, withdrawal, anger, resentment, bitterness, angina, along with the whole sleuth of other emotional and physical issues and disorders. In the mind of most children of the enslaved ancestors, there is a genuine and constant awareness of how quickly life can change, along with the never-ending struggle to overcome a society that takes every opportunity to remind you of your skin color through obstacles in career ascension, housing equity, employment equality, healthcare disparity, and equal justice in due process. This while doing your best to present a happy-go-lucky demeanor, not to upset your oppressor.

This type of atmosphere, if subjected to it long enough, produces a kind of self-identity that is almost always harmful to the person. The only way the immature mind can overcome it is through aggression at any resistance. I mean that you can only beat a person for so long before they begin to defend themselves and their family aggressively. The gospel has something to say about oppressive and lording-over behavior. But before we explore that, I want to bring us back to the church in the south and, more importantly, the ecclesia and their notable absence during all of this. Jesus asked us to understand the needs and feelings of the oppressed, defend them, stand up for them, and help them.

Psalm 9:9 *"The LORD is a stronghold for the oppressed, a stronghold in times of trouble."*

Proverbs 14:31 *"Whoever oppresses a poor man insults his Maker, but he who is generous to the needy honors him."*

Isaiah 1: 17, *"Learn to do good; seek justice, correct oppression; bring justice to the fatherless, plead the widow's cause."*

Psalm 34: 18 says, *"The LORD is near to the brokenhearted and saves the crushed in spirit."*

Zechariah 7:10, *"Do not oppress the widow, the fatherless, the sojourner, or the poor, and let none of you devise evil against another in your heart."*

Luke 4: 18-19, *"The Spirit of the Lord is upon me*

*because he has anointed me to proclaim good news to the poor. He has sent me to proclaim liberty to the captives and recovering of sight to the blind, to set at liberty those who are oppressed, to proclaim the year of the Lord's favor."*

Malachi 3:5, *"Then I will draw near to you for judgment. I will be a swift witness against the sorcerers, against the adulterers, against those who swear falsely, against those who oppress the hired worker in his wages, the widow and the fatherless, against those who thrust aside the sojourner, and do not fear me, says the LORD of hosts."*

The gospel asked us to submit to those who have ruled over us, but it never asked us to participate in immoral and sinful behavior with those same rulers. Some of these very scriptures were never read by the enslaved Africans because they could not read, and most could not because of their oppressors. However, even the ones who could read, like the local enslaved pastors, still would not have read these scriptures because they were forced to read from the "UNHOLY Slave›s Bible," which only had thirty-two of the sixty-six books of the King James Bible. Only fourteen of the thirty-nine Old Testament books and eighteen of the twenty-seven New Testament books. Even God's word was not sacred enough for this church to enslave and violate the scriptures. Deuteronomy 4:2 says, *"You shall not add to the word which I command you, nor take from it, that you may keep the commandments of the* LORD *your God which I command you."*

## The 13ᵗʰ 14ᵗʰ and 15ᵗʰ Amendments

Better known as the reconstruction amendments. The era between 1865 and 1870 is known as the historical reconstruction era of the confederacy. The 13ᵗʰ amendment officially abolished slavery in the United States of America; the 14ᵗʰ amendment gave the enslaved people of Africa full citizenship in America, due process, and equal protection under the law of the land. The 15ᵗʰ amendment gave African men only the right to vote in 1870. In 1857, a Supreme Court case known as the Dred Scott Decision determined that black Americans were not citizens. The Fourteenth Amendment overturned that ruling, stating, 'All persons born or naturalized in the United States are citizens of the United States and the State where they reside.' This was one of three Constitutional amendments to establish political equality for Americans of any race.

The goal of the 13th amendment was the abolishment of slavery throughout the country and its territories. We know this did not happen all at once, as we know about the Galveston, Texas incident we now celebrate as Juneteenth, which President Biden signed into law as a Federal Holiday in 2022. On December 6th, 1865, the amendment was passed into law, and it reads, "neither slavery nor involuntary servitude, except as a punishment for the crime of whom the party shall have been duly convicted, shall exist within the United States, or any place subject to their jurisdiction.' The exception that allows servitude as punishment for a crime will enable prisons to use inmate labor."

The goal of the 14ᵗʰ amendment was to provide equal rights to the people of the United States. Passed by Congress on June 13, 1866, and ratified on July 9, 1868, the 14ᵗʰ Amendment extended liberties and rights granted by the Bill of Rights to formerly enslaved people. Following the Civil War, Congress submitted to the states three amendments as part of its Reconstruction program to guarantee equal civil and legal rights to Black citizens. A significant provision of the 14ᵗʰ Amendment was to grant citizenship to "All persons born or naturalized in the United States," thereby giving citizenship to formerly enslaved people. Another equally important provision was that "no state deprives any person of life, liberty, or property, without due process of law; nor deny to any person within its jurisdiction the equal protection of the laws." The right to due process of law and equal protection of the law is now applied to the federal and state governments.

On June 16, 1866, the House Joint Resolution

proposing the 14th Amendment to the Constitution was submitted to the states. On July 28, 1868, the 14th amendment was declared, in a certificate of the Secretary of State, ratified by the necessary 28 of the 37 States, and became part of the supreme law of the land.[9]

The goal of the 15th amendment was to grant African American men, formerly enslaved people, the right to vote. Passed by Congress on February 26, 1869, and ratified on February 3, 1870, the 15th Amendment granted African American men the right to vote. To former abolitionists and the Radical Republicans in Congress who fashioned Reconstruction after the Civil War, the 15th Amendment, enacted in 1870, appeared to signify the fulfillment of all promises to African Americans. Set free by the 13th amendment, with citizenship guaranteed by the 14th Amendment, The 15th Amendment gave black males the vote.

In retrospect, the 15th Amendment was only another step in the struggle for equality that would continue

---

9    Milestone Documents. National Archives 02/08/2022

for more than a century before African Americans could fully participate in American public and civic life. African Americans exercised the right to vote and held office in many Southern states through the 1880s. In the early 1890s, steps were taken to ensure subsequent "white supremacy." Literacy tests for the vote, "grandfather clauses" excluding from the franchise all whose ancestors had not voted in the 1860s, and other devices to disenfranchise African Americans were written into the laws of former Confederate states.

Social and economic segregation was added to Black America's loss of political power. In 1896, the Supreme Court decision *Plessy* v. *Ferguson* legalized "separate but equal" facilities for the races. For more than 50 years, the overwhelming majority of African American citizens were reduced to second-class citizenship under the "Jim Crow" segregation system. During that time, African Americans sought to secure their rights and improve their position through organizations such as the National Association for the Advancement of Colored People and the National Urban League and the individual efforts of reformers like Booker T. Washington, W.E.B. DuBois, and A. Philip Randolph.

The most direct attack on the problem of African American disenfranchisement came in 1965. Prompted by reports of continuing discriminatory voting practices in many Southern states, President Lyndon B. Johnson, himself a southerner, urged Congress on March 15, 1965, to pass legislation "which will make it impossible to thwart the 15th Amendment." He reminded Congress that "we cannot have a government for all the people until we first make certain it is the government of and by all the people."

The Voting Rights Act of 1965, extended in 1970, 1975, and 1982, abolished all remaining deterrents to exercising the right to vote and authorized federal supervision of voter registration where necessary. In 2013, the Supreme Court struck down a key provision of the act involving federal oversight of voting rules in nine states.[10]

---

10  Ibid.

As stated in an earlier chapter, a segment of this country's society has endured and passed down through the generations a historical, ideological belief soaked in violence, hate, and racism. Today, this segment has latched on to the Republican Party and openly proclaimed loathing for foreigners, immigrants, and the minority. They were successful at stemming the advancements of the reconstruction era from 1865 -1870; this group denied a woman her right to vote until the 19th amendment in 1919 and instituted "Jim Crow" and segregation laws to continue to oppress and disenfranchise African American citizens and forty-eight years after the civil rights act of 1965 they were able to get a conservative Supreme Court to restrict a key benefit to that law severely. As the country becomes more democratic and centered politically, this group becomes more emboldened in rhetoric, calling for a second American Revolution or the rise of the Confederacy. And while most of this is just free speech venting, there is a real effort to stack state-elected positions with candidates who share this societal and White Christian Nationalist view of the country and world. So, they have power over the Electoral College. They call themselves MAGA.

## The Law of Race

After one-hundred-plus years of fighting this ideology of segregation and separation by race, we find it still alive and well in our society due to our federal government's genuine and legal efforts. In his book "The Color of Law," Professor and Fellow Richard Rothstein reveals this hidden truth about our government over the last one hundred years: the creation of nothing less than our very own apartheid system here in America in the public and private housing market.[11] This malicious activity has a long history in our country, just as long as we have existed, and the church has been right there as a witness and, in some cases, as an active participant. According to Rothstein, from 2014 to 2016, when our

---

11  Richard Rothstein. The Color of Law, Liveright Publishing Corporation New York, NY 2017. Preface

country was ablaze with civil unrest due to the numerous high-profile killings of young African American men in places like Ferguson, Mo., Baltimore, Ma., Milwaukee, WI., and Charlotte, NC., showed us what we thought we knew, how these segregated neighborhoods, with their crime, violence, anger, and poverty came to be. We said these neighborhoods were the way they were because of "de facto segregation" from private practices, not governmental policy.

"De Facto Segregation" dictates that as black families move into white neighborhoods like Ferguson and racially minded white families begin to leave, more black families move in. "White flight" becomes real, along with the neighborhood's deterioration. Real estate firms steer black families away from white communities and white families away from black ones. Banks and lending institutions discriminate through redlining and refusing to give mortgages to African Americans or extracting unusually severe terms from them for subprime loans. This is what we know to be the reality. But some, if not all, of these activities, would still be present in our history but would not be so prevalent, insidious, and bold without federal approval and support.

## Hiding in Plain Sight

De facto segregation is a smoke screen over a much deeper problem that goes back to 1883 and a US Supreme Court ruling. As previously spoken, the 13th, 14th, and 15th amendments were considered the reconstruction amendments as they sought to right the wrongs of slavery. The 13th amendment abolished slavery for formerly enslaved people in all aspects of life in America. Still, in 1883 the US Supreme Court rejected the notion of section 2 of that amendment as they believed that housing was not a badge or incident of slavery and was not under the amendment nor the "Civil Rights Act of 1866", which, in turn, kept African Americans in second-class status as citizens and continued the relics of slavery. This continued into the 1960s with the passing of the Fair Housing Act of

1965 and its expansion in 1968.

It amounted to not de facto segregation but rather the court's terminology of de jure: segregation by law and public policy. In other words, our de jure segregation is because of laws, not de facto because we like living apart from one another.

# CHAPTER 7

# MAKE AMERICA GREAT AGAIN MOVEMENT
# (MAGA)

*John 14: 5-6*

*"Thomas said to Him, 'Lord, we do not know where you are going, and how can we know the way?' Jesus told him, ' I am the way, the truth, and the life. No one comes to the Father except through me.'"*

## What is the MAGA Movement?

The "Make America Great Again" movement is a political catchphrase that came to prominence in the 2016 presidential election race between President Donald Trump and Hilary Clinton. This slogan transformed into a political campaign and, ultimately, Christian nationalism. The oxymoronic aspect of Christian nationalism is that it believes in and exports an ideology and doctrine of exclusion that is rebranded into self-love of the country first. MAGA further insinuates what America should look like through racial identity and blind political allegiance towards the Republican Party.

The movement has attracted and welcomed many fringe groups that espouse a racial separatist manifesto, such as the "Alt-Right Movement" and "KKK." It has also attracted subgroups that espoused violently racist and anti-Muslim doctrines like the "Proud Boys," "Oath Keepers," and "Qanon." These groups are drawn to the

MAGA movement's Christian nationalist message of exclusion. MAGA can best be described as a gathering place in the public square for free speech to emotionally preach the grievances of the human heart and turn to age-old attitudes of racism, anti-Semitism, sexism, and violence to intimidate and violently bring the ideology into national existence. The MAGA Christian Nationalist message contradicts the Gospel of Jesus Christ message.

The national Jewish leadership and the international Roman Empire put Christ on the cross as both were threatened by his message of repentance, love, and inclusion. At its core, the gospel message incorporates, without limits and or judgments, the unity of inclusive capitalism, socialism, and the oneness of faith and humanity. Conversely, MAGA strives for division. To thin out the herd, so to speak so, individual and group achievements can be bestowed on an exclusive white majority, and recognition and reward are easier to access. All our systems have been set up to identify our race, ethnicity, and gender differences through census surveys, job applications, financial background checks, taxes, and the like. The MAGA movement is not new, but it has found a way to penetrate and release what has already been in the human heart. Jeremiah 17:9-10 *"The heart is deceitful above all things and desperately wicked; who can know it. I, the Lord, search the heart; I test the mind. Even to give every man according to his ways and the fruits of his doings."*

## The Politics of Race & Religion

The root of this type of politics is based on manipulations and lies. Its goal is to use racial, religious, climate, or any other crises to divide people along lines, and in many cases, the situation tends to match the race. So anti-abortion politics look for white Christian evangelicals and then try to empower them through scripture to behave in specific ways that will get the political figure and the message the most media exposure. This is the same playbook for racial politics, especially in minority communities. Where people of color feel under-represented, so they actively cast ballots based on race or ethnicity. Ironically, practicing this behavior in the workplace and classroom is illegal, even though it happens far too much in American corporations. So, the same elected officials who get elected on racial and religious politics are now enforcing laws that prohibit and prosecute it in other industries in America.

Another irony as it pertains to evangelicals for me is that I have always found that the best form of evangelism is not handing out tracks to strangers or blocking family planning centers but rather a behavior. If you want people to listen to the passions of your heart, treat them nicely, especially if they don't look like you or are of a different ethnic background. This is the message of the Good Samaritan biblical story. This type of politics can be extremely violent and deadly when sectarian violence is used, as we have witnessed in Muslim countries like Saudi Arabia, Pakistan, India, Afghanistan, Somalia, Turkey, Rwanda, and Nigeria.

In these societies, there is usually a difference in the orthodoxies of the faith, as in Suina's practice of Islam as to the Shite's practice of it. Or one religion over another, as in American Christianity over Islam in America or certain European countries like Sweden. Then there are the outliers with a duality of religious fanaticism and terrorist manifestos, such as Boko Haram, Al-Qaeda, and the Taliban. Not all politics of religion are politically based; some are deeply rooted in the doctrine of the faith of its believers. In America, the Amish communities of Pennsylvania still practice some form of isolation and separation from the modern world. They believe doing this will reduce their exposure to sin and temptation in the larger society, which can consume their communities and distract them from focusing their energy on their own families and community. The Amish incorporated this doctrine from the arrival to the new world as the "Anabaptist faith."

In Brooklyn, NY, a few orthodox Jewish communities practice politics by religion using a combination of doctrine and religious identity politics. They are:

- Lubavitcher community in Crown Heights Brooklyn

- Hasidic community in Williamsburg Brooklyn

- Hasidic Orthodox community in Borough Park Brooklyn

- Modern Orthodox community in Midwood Brooklyn

- Sephardic Kings community in Gravesend Brooklyn

## The Division of a Society

America has never been a united society; from its inception, there were divisions and dividing forces in the forms of countries like England, France, and

Spain, along with the internal details of greed, power, religion, and race. This was natural as we have never been monolithic.

But rather a polylithic society. If we have ever been united, it's been around an ideology of America and the life that ideology promises to those who believe. But America is also transactional, and the highest bidders tend to get the best parts of that ideology. These divisions were terrible enough, but people got used to them and expected them; as the norm, the MAGA ideology has added another dynamic to the mix, which is purposeful and willful to be divisive for the division's sake. Meaning people will make the most harmful decisions for themselves and others to be opposite from anyone they deem an anti-MAGA movement.

As the world is in recovery from the global COVID-19 pandemic, we as an international community have suffered tremendously through loss of life, whether it be family members, close friends, spouses, or children. The death toll has been so significant that it almost seemed like every remaining living person knew someone who died directly or indirectly from this virus. Yet when we had chances to limit exposure and spread of the virus through face mask wearing and lockdowns, certain southern and mid-western states and cities whose populations identified as majority republican and with the MAGA movement blatantly disobeyed federal and state public health orders and began to open up for business as usual the most dangerous places to themselves and others. These acts were highly political and costly to the lives of all, but it was all political theater and fuel for the MAGA movement.

## The Media: Fake News or Mouthpiece of the Movement

Since the inception of the news media, they have had one foundational rule: "If it bleeds, it leads." this North Star has led them into a journalistic and political quagmire, and they can't seem to find their way out. A movement like the MAGA movement that touches on all the trigger points appears to have been made for this atmosphere of local, national, and international news coverage, where they get front page and nightly lead stories while also being on the 24/7 cable news loop cycle. As they bring the racial, religious, ethnic, and geographical conflict to the viewers' homes, office computers, and smartphones at the speed of desires and addictions, they obsessively critique the divisive turn the country and the world have taken.

What is responsible journalism? What is the Cronkite standard? Where do you find it? And how can it become relevant again with so much lustful greed involved in the hearts of the so-called watchers of society? Can a news outlet be objective when they face the pressures to be first to break the story, rating metrics, celebrity-minded and egotistical anchors, and the never-ending allure of corporate and individual fame through worldwide recognition? I think not. But, before I get too deep into the whys and why-not of the Media's internal missions and the conflicts it creates, let's get back to the operational behavior and how that behavior, either through being manipulated or clear-thinking commission, gives us the same outcomes. All media outlets reporting on the MAGA movement have directly or indirectly become its mouthpiece. What's fake or not fake all depends on us, the viewers, and what outlets we watch. Now proponents of the media will say that I'm misguided because the press did not start the message, they report it, or they don't make the news; they report it. But if a tree falls in the woods and no one hears it, did it fall? The point being made is that the news media bears some responsibility for the state of divisiveness in America because but not for the media, the MAGA movement would have never become so widespread, so insidious, and so influential or disgusting in the hearts and minds of many Americans.

# CHAPTER 8

# GOVERNMENT OF, FOR, AND BY

*Isaiah 9:6*

*For unto us a Child is born, unto us a Son is given; And the government will be upon His shoulder. And His name will be called Wonderful, Counselor, Mighty God, Everlasting Father, Prince of Peace.*

## What is a Government System?

A primary government system is a political body elected by its people to represent them to distribute power and authority among different levels of a state. This work on behalf of the people is done to improve the people's lives in quality, organization, safety, financial security, and sovereignty. But should government see itself as working for the people or babysitting the people? The "Nanny State" is a term that originated in the United Kingdom. It represents a new government module that overregulates people's lives through policies to control personal behavior related to health and lifestyle choices. In New York City over the last twenty-two years, we have seen this on display through the policies of the previous three mayors. It starts with Mayor Michael Bloomberg through Bill De Blasio and current Mayor Eric Adams. Beginning in 2006, the administration banned trans fats in all restaurants, which affected many businesses and catering services. Mayor Bloomberg even went as far as to try to ban "Big Gulp" soda drinks. These mayors have removed all vending machines that serve sodas and snacks like potato chips, chocolate bars, and nuts, and replaced them with devices that serve water and trans-fat-free snacks. Mayor Adams recently changed the city schools' breakfast and lunch plans and the public health system's patient meal plans. All of these policies seem to be in the people's best interest. But people should be allowed to make choices that they feel are best for their own health.

New York City is so overregulated that in its effort to protect its citizens, they compromise said citizens constitutionally protected freedoms. In 2022 the United States Supreme Court ruled that New York City and State gun laws were unconstitutional and gave all New Yorkers the right to apply for concealed gun carrying permits. Since there was no way to appeal the ruling, the governor of the state and the mayor of New York City tried to limit the spaces for a person to carry a loaded concealed gun. They have regulated that you can only take a concealed handgun in your home and property, but most NYC streets, parks, and public spaces are off-limits. The "Nanny State" does not realize that specific laws are oppressive and unnecessary as they compromise liberty, solidarity, and responsibility. It almost always turns the citizen off as they turn their backs on this governing, and they choose not to participate in any aspect of it, from voting to jury duty. But a more dire issue occurs from the "Nanny State," when the government fails to ask or inform the people on how it spends their money, where it spends their money, and on whom they spend it. My point here is that the "Nanny State" can be just as oppressive in the twenty-first century as the confederacy was in the eighteenth, no matter how good the intentions.

## American Government

The American Government system is based on the

notion that government should be of the people, for the people, and by the people meaning the citizenry should be active participants in how their country, state, city, town, or village is being governed. This system has been flawed because term limits were not built into all federal, state, and local government election offices. Candidates, except for a few offices, can stay in office for a lifetime if they can keep getting elected. This is easy to do with the inception of lobbyists, Super PACs, and dark money, which are the illegal funds that flow into campaign coffers with no point of origin and no way to trace those funds flowing into all levels of elections to buy elected officials. Even though American Democracy was launched on the loftiest of ideals. It didn't stay there for very long; the question I always asked is why people spend so much time, effort, and money to win political offices. A statistical summary of the last twenty-four-month campaigns of the 2019 -2020 election cycle revealed the following numbers:

- Presidential Candidates raised and spent $4.1 billion

- Congressional Candidates collected approximately $4.1 billion and disbursed approximately $3.8 billion

- Political Parties received $3.2 billion and spent $3 billion

- Political Action Committees (PACs) raised approximately $13.2 billion and spent $12.9 billion

What is the draw to achieving this? What is the pot of gold at the end of the campaign rainbow? And it looks like the pot of gold is us, the people. Fred Hampton, a former leader of the Black Panther Party, had a catchphrase that said, "People Power" if you have the people, you have the power.

## Predatory Capitalism

Where capitalism is an economic system where the production of goods and services are privately owned and operated for profit in a free market structure, predatory capitalism is something completely different. In this environment, markets and industries are free from government regulations and usher in a culture of greed and insatiable opportunities for the super-rich as they prey on the lower classes for profit. This is not a free race to the bottom in a zero-sum game for maximum profits only as in **"Ruthless Capitalism,"** but rather a cooperating of government regulators and industries working together to generate maximum profits at the expense of safety regulations that protect the public.

An example is the Boeing Aircraft manufacturer and their 737 MAX jetliners. The issue with this product revolves around two tragic airline accidents in five months, Lion Air flight 610 crashed on October 29th, 2018, in the "Java Sea" which killed all of its 189 passengers, and Ethiopian Airlines flight 302 crashed on March 10th, 2019, in Ethiopia six minutes after takeoff killing all of its 157 passengers. All Boeing 737 MAX jetliners were grounded worldwide for twenty-one months. Between the whistleblower reports, Congressional, Justice Department, and FBI investigation, Boeing settled and accepted full responsibility for the crashes due to plant and production problems. They paid fines in the billions. What was also revealed was the incompetence and complacency of the FAA in its oversight of Boeing and its rush to clear Boeing and get the 737 Max jetliner back in the air. In this case, the FAA's lack of regulatory oversight allowed Boeing to rush planes through the assembly process to fill back orders and be competitive in the industry at the expense of the general public's safety. In this case, the American government's federal aviation oversight body was not working for the people but directly or indirectly for Boeing and its shareholders; this is classic predatory capitalism. As we look at American Democracy versus Biblical Theocracy, a stark difference begins to take shape even if we limit our vision to the scripture in Isaiah chapter 9.

## Leader or Servant Leader

These prophetic verses of our soon-coming king give a detailed and descriptive insight into life under the Biblical Jesus. Man can never be equal to God, but a man should always try to be Christ-like in word and deeds (Philippians 2:5 *"Let this mind be in you, which was also in Christ Jesus"*), *"For unto us a Child is born, unto us, a Son is given; and the government will be upon His shoulder. And His name will be Wonderful, Counselor, Mighty God, Everlasting Father, and Prince of Peace."* Governments should always be supportive, protective, comforting, and peaceful towards their citizens in how they govern. The spiritual dynamic in a theocracy is the development of the citizen to reach inward and exercise all available gifts and talents given to the individual for the collective benefit of the body/humanity.

When government policies advocate for "Ruthless and Predatory Capitalism," some segments of society will be victimized, damaged, and even destroyed. These segments are almost always poor and minority, so how does the individual who is poor and a minority insulate their heart and emotions while at the same time liberating their minds from such evil governance? The key here is to ensure you are not becoming your oppressor in thoughts and behaviors. This is where Jesus's saying about rendering unto Caesar what is his only and God what is his. So, if God is getting the sinful heart for repentance, then Caesar will benefit from the redeeming work of Christ. Ephesians 2:10 *"For we are His workmanship, created in Christ Jesus for good works, which God prepared beforehand that we should walk in them."* When humanity gives in to its desires, bad things happen on the planet, for every unrepentant heart thinks they are right in its own eyes. Our society has needed examples of servant leadership from its inception. We have been bombarded with greed and lust beyond measure from the church house to the Whitehouse; our insatiable appetite to promote self has made us weak to the desire of the flesh and eyes and have succumbed to our prideful hearts and terrible tongues. The evidence looks clear and convincing that after two hundred and forty-six years of established government authority and living under an established legal document, we as a society seem to be devolving into a cesspool of divisive ideologies, selfish political viewpoints communicated through aggressive hateful speech, and violent behavior.

Beloved, this didn't happen by happenchance but progressed gradually like a deceptive underwater current taking us out into deep waters. Even the most jaded among us seemed concerned about where our society and humanity are heading and whether we can right this ethos. Independence fuels pride, pride breeds division and conflict, and conflict leads to chaos, but dependency lets us off the hook in knowing that this battle is not ours; all we are responsible for is trust and obedience. Proverbs 3: 5-6 *"Trust in the Lord with all your heart, and lean not on your understanding; in all your ways acknowledge Him, and He shall direct your path."*

If we could only get out of our ways, this could be a way out of our current quagmire.

## Power

The real power lies with the one "who decides what gets decided," but strength not tempered with mercy tends to corrupt. Let us look at American ingenuity and, by default, American corporations, both private and public. Over the last ten years, I had the pleasure of writing a three-book trilogy on corporate America and its coexistence with Christianity as a faith and way of life. America is the greatest nation ever established on earth due, in fact, to its ingenuity and its ability to come together and imagine what can be. American corporations, along with their government partners, have led the way in transforming daily life and society from agricultural to industrial to technological and, along the way, created the most excellent economy humanity has ever seen. And somewhere along the way, we lost our decency for one another and went from creative partners and co-laborers to competitors and work adversaries.

How did this happen, and why? The love and pursuit of money occupy a significant part of American life because, in America, money gives you social power that penetrates and operates at all levels of American society (formal, informal, legitimate, and illegitimate). The heiress and the mobster can eat at the same restaurants, fly first class and live in the most affluent neighborhoods because the power of money affords social exclusivity and affluence. Another preoccupation in American life is controlling the ability to control one's life and time. Some believe you need to be able to manipulate others to get more control of yourself. In the prism of office politics, power and control are practiced immaturely.

It is used exclusively to coerce, force, and influence in scenarios like sexual harassment or financial and ethical corruption. The power of control can lead to abusive, intimidating, and overbearing behavior.

Still, power can be displayed without control, especially if it is turned inward to overcome character flaws, insecurities, and negative proclivities, which has led us to this current state in the workforce. CNBC's new report citing a 2022 Gallup "State of the Global Workplace 2022" found "Sixty percent of people reported being emotionally detached at work and 19% as being miserable. Only 33% reported feeling engaged, and that is even lower than in 2020. In the U.S. specifically, 50% of workers reported feeling stressed at their jobs daily, 41% as being worried, 22% as sad, and 18% as angry. Fifty percent of the US workforce are in jobs they are stressed by and spend up to eight to ten hours a day; at those jobs, this data may correlate with the current "Great Resignation" period we find ourselves in.

# CHAPTER 9

# CHICKENS COMING HOME TO ROOST

*Galatians 6: 6-9*

*Let him who is taught the word share in all good*
*things with him who teaches. Do not be deceived;*
*God is not mocked; whatever a man sows, he will reap. He*
*who sows to his flesh will of the flesh reap corruption, but*
*he who sows to the Spirit will of the Spirit reap everlasting*
*life. And let us not grow weary while doing well, for, in due*
*season, we shall reap if we do not lose heart.*

## Control or Witchcraft

For America, the saying "the chickens have come home to roost" has always represented past wrong deeds that have come back to cause present-day problems. This saying was made famous or infamous by Malcolm X, the charismatic leader of the Nation of Islam. When he used it to summarize the assassination of President John F. Kennedy. In my counseling practice in "Corporate America," some of the most common disorders I counseled staff were fear, anxiety, and burnout, followed closely by depression and discouragement. Most stem from a combination of workplace trauma and dissatisfaction with where they are in their careers.

A significant number of them are caught in the "Stuck Disorder." In a previous chapter, I wrote about a penetrating ethos, meaning a powerful and enticing spiritual characteristic that grabs the attention of all and infects most with its lust for more. This deceptive characteristic, along with the manipulation of the corporate elite, deceives people into believing they can have it all and have it all now. In the world today and as it has always been in recent history, people celebrate and idolize those with "more," whether it be riches, material possessions, position, or access. We tend to measure our lives as meaningful, purposeful, and worthy based on the material success that can be measured, quantified, and balanced. And this always seems to lead us into the pursuit of and competing with to acquire.

But what's more dangerous is the internal psychology and value we place on ourselves if we don't have as much of or more than the next person. Once this mental ideology has been established in our hearts, the battlefield operation of the 'chickens coming home to roost' can be implemented. We often behave in these manners so subconsciously that it seems natural and feels justified. In our marred history as a society and in addition to the committed atrocities of slavery, we have saddled and burdened others into caste status, labeled our entire culture based on financial worth as to who is upper class, middle class, and lower class, subjected people to treatment becoming of their course and station in life. We even have churches, "Houses of God," publicly boasting of how many millionaires are members of their congregation, along with the subtle invitation to join them in this lifestyle by "living your best life now."

You may hear things like "God does not want you poor, stressed, anxious, or bound." These can be very enticing to the faint of heart and weak in faith because they can rearrange your constitution and turn you into something completely different from God's design through inspired scripture in the life of the believers. It can stir up the competitive juices in our hearts and live our lives in a zero-sum game mindset, with the winner taking all the spoils. Here we find the profit over people doctrine, where mass layoffs live, downsizing corporations live, and export jobs to poorer nations to save on labor costs by paying subsistent wages. In turn, it forces the American worker to compete more aggressively to get and keep employment by displaying all manner of dishonorable and unethical behaviors and turns our workplaces into breeding grounds of fear & anxiety, stress, and disgust in an atmosphere of quiet quitting. In other words, "we are reaping what we have sown" or "the chickens have come home to roost."

**2 Timothy 3: 16-17** *"All Scripture is given by inspiration of God, and is profitable for doctrine, for reproof, for correction, for instruction in righteousness, that the man of God may be complete, thoroughly equipped for every good work."*

God-inspired scripture is a blessing to one's life, for it brings peace from within, contentment in our positions and status, and fulfillment from labor. It has never been designed to make us rich, famous, influential, or great leaders. These things come from the heart of man. And because man's heart is, as scripture describes, "Deceitfully Wicked," our behavior displays this wickedness when desires are delayed or denied. Jealousy, envy, corruption, violence, oppression, and manipulation can fill the heart because the heart wants what it wants, and rarely will it take no for an answer.

People use control as an insurance policy to bring their desires to fruition. If situations and people can be controlled into doing the things that benefit the controller, then the scheme has worked. So, in the end, is this control, or is it witchcraft? This question will have to be answered by society. Still, to get to the actual answer, humanity will have to go through many trials and tribulations as people have gone through individually to see the truth. A servant is not greater than his master; if they crucified and killed the master, why won't the servant be in jeopardy?

## Control and Creativity

All human beings want to be in control of their lives, especially their creativity and its manifestations. When our creative juices are flowing, we become alive. It is the one gift/characteristic God has given us that is equal to him on a smaller scale. The ability to create something from our imagination out of nothing is an excellent work of our humanity. In the very first words of the Hebrew Bible, it says, *"In the beginning, God Created..."*

We are introduced to God amid his creative work as we are also <u>part</u> of that work. So, you can imagine how one might feel to have their creative gifts controlled by others and, in some cases, stolen. Our history is filled with citizens suffering these affronts and offenses. Even the American church has fallen into the grips of Satan in their desire to be famous and well-known with the hope that it will attract parishioners who then become tithe-paying members. To accomplish this, the church finds itself at the mercy of the marketing industry of the twenty-first century.

Because in America, fame sells and popularity lusts after it; in this world where our reality is constantly competing with an exploding virtual reality, people are lusting after and gravitating more and more at lightning speed to live in and have their desires fulfilled in this virtual space because it allows them a life beyond their circumstances and limitations. It even allows them a lucrative career if they are seen enough and have many others willing to follow. The way it works is that one must become famous or infamous to get to popularity or notoriety to catch the eye of the public. The famous achieve this through great talent at their craft, mainly in the entertainment, sports, or political industry; the infamous achieve this through bizarre and, in some cases, explicit and demeaning behavior. But these lines sometimes cross over when the famous become infamous and the infamous become famous. When this is achieved, you become an influencer in virtual reality, and marketing agencies seek you out to promote their clients, organizations, and/or products. This book may also have to dabble in this industry to generate sales.

My point here is that the power of your creativity may no longer be under your control if you must compromise it for fame and financial rewards. This is how many inventors, authors, painters, and creators have had their ideas stolen, swindled, or buried over the history of America, and now we find what is supposed to be our most sacred institution joined at the hip with these practices to satisfy their desires. Some may say, "pastor, you are not being fair," and exaggerate the point. But, still, if men can be accused of watching pornography as contributing to human trafficking and the sex slave industry, which may very well be accurate, what's the difference when the church abandons millennia of ecumenical evangelism through ministries of help, compassion, and behavior in the local community and the satisfaction of that call in their vineyard to now market themselves around the world to people they will never meet and who will never enter their sanctuaries? If your gifts are not a blessing in your local community first, how can they be a blessing elsewhere? And what about the local church in that community on the other side of the world that is already doing kingdom business and depends on the offerings and contributions of their parishioners; is it right for God's people to comport

125

themselves in such a worldly manner? Well, God has something to say about that.

God sent the prophet Nathan to confront King David for this same greedy and selfish behavior in 2 Samuel 12: 1-9 *"Then the LORD sent Nathan to David. And he came to him and said: "There were two men in one city, one rich and the other poor. The rich man had exceedingly many flocks and herds. But the poor man had nothing except one little ewe lamb, which he had bought and nourished, and it grew up together with him and his children. It ate of his food, drank from his cup, and lay in his bosom, and it was like a daughter to him. And a traveler came to the rich man, who refused to take from his flock and from his herd to prepare one for the wayfaring man who had come to him; but he took the poor man's lamb and prepared it for the man who had come to him. "So David's anger was greatly aroused against the man, and he said to Nathan, "As the LORD lives, the man who has done this shall surely die! And he shall restore fourfold for the lamb because he did this and had no pity."*

*Then Nathan said to David, "You are the man! Thus says the LORD God of Israel: 'I anointed you king over Israel, and I delivered you from the hand of Saul. I gave you your master's house and your master's wives into your keeping and gave you the house of Israel and Judah. And if that had been too little, I would have given you much more! Why have you despised the commandment of the LORD to do evil in His sight? You have killed Uriah the Hittite with the sword; you have taken his wife to be your wife and have killed him with the sword of the people of Ammon."*

## Control and Productivity

Like stealing a person's ideas, stealing their credit, reward, or accolades can be even worse. Sometimes in life, people take credit for things and accomplishments they have not done, and in most cases, it just amounts to lying. The practice is so common that it has become accepted in society. Many people lie on their resumes, embellish their previous job responsibilities, and take credit for projects they did not work on or were involved with.

What is even worse is how widespread and perverse the practice has become. Even worse and more dangerous is when it is done in real-time to real people.

At the 2016 Republican national convention and the 2018 "Be Best campaign," First Lady Melania Trump gave speeches where she was caught plagiarizing two First Lady Michelle Obama's speeches. This public embarrassment forced Mrs. Trump and her staff to apologize for the confusion; if fact checkers were not looking, this insult would have gone unchecked. But what about the millions of middle managers, admin assistants, and assistant managers who submit monthly, quarterly, and annual productive reports to their department heads who just put their names on the information and fast track it up to the top floor and take all the credit for everyone else's hard work? This seems to be the standard operating procedure in corporate America. Even our political candidates are not immune from this desire to be more. In the state of NY, a 2022 congressional candidate lied so egregiously during his campaign to win a congressional seat. The lies were so shockingly outlandish that they might very well permanently damage his character, reputation, and ability to find gainful employment.

# CHAPTER 10

# THE FUTURE

# ECCLESIASTICAL AND CIVIL AUTHORITY

*Daniel 2:41–43*

*"Whereas you saw the feet and toes, partly of potter's clay and partly of iron, the kingdom shall be divided; yet the strength of the iron shall be in it, just as you saw the iron mixed with ceramic clay. And as the toes of the feet were partly of iron and partly of clay, so the kingdom shall be partly strong and partly fragile. As you saw iron mixed with ceramic clay, they will mingle with the seed of men; but they will not adhere to one another, just as iron does not mix with clay."*

## Who Granted the Bishop of Rome Universal Authority?

Before I dive into Roman history, let's build a little context around Daniel's prophecy. His vision has taken us to the end times of human history, which places us at the feet of the statue, not just the feet but at the ten toes. Here we see a mixing of clay and iron. The clay represents the New Testament church set free at Pentecost, and the iron represents Roman political power and pagan culture. The Christian church will be integrated with Roman politics and paganism.

Daniel 2:41 *"Whereas you saw the feet and toes, partly of potter's clay and partly of iron, the kingdom shall be divided; yet the strength of the iron shall be in it, just as you saw the iron mixed with ceramic clay."*

The church began to mix with the political power of Rome and Roman pagan beliefs. In the first five hundred years of church history, when the cannons were being formulated into the "Bible," the church found itself on the outskirts of society and civil discourse. It was regulated to a home-based scattered entity with no organized rules or doctrines. This changed in 313 A.D. when Roman Emperors Constantine 1 and Licinius drafted the "Edict of Milan." This proclamation permanently established religious toleration for Christianity throughout the Roman Empire. It granted Christian's the freedom to assemble and organize churches along with the return of all confiscated property. Before this, in 306 A.D. Emperor Constantine converted to Christianity, believing that the Christian God helped him win a series of civil war battles to conquer Rome and become Emperor. History states that Constantine received a vision from God where an Angel told him that he must defeat with the sign of the cross. During the reign of Emperor Constantine, Christians went from being persecuted to holding positions of influence and power in the courts and palaces of kings and governors. Becoming a Christian was an excellent choice to advance in the military or imperial civil service positions. As the people of the Roman Empire converted, they brought along with them their former pagan beliefs, and the intermingling continued. Pagan statues were renamed after Biblical figures:

- Jupiter became the Apostle Peter

- The Madonna and child became the virgin Mary and baby Jesus

- Pagan worship of the sun became Sunday worship for the church instead of the biblical Sabbath.

- Note, all the other days of the week were transitioned out of Paganism and into the names we currently know them by: Moon Day became Monday, Tiw's Day became Tuesday, Wodens' Day became Wednesday, Thor's Day became Thursday, Fríge's Day became Friday, and Saturn's Day became Saturday.

## How Did the Church Get Civil Authority?

When Emperor Constantine moved his empire from Rome to Constantinople, the Bishop of Rome was left in charge of the western empire. In 538 AD, Emperor Justinian gave a decree acknowledging the Bishop of Rome as the head of all churches. In the same year, the Roman church was given political, civil, and ecclesiastical power. Now the word Papacy is being used to describe the Bishop of Rome; The Papacy was given all religious, political, and civil administration of Rome. From AD 351 to AD 476, the Roman Empire was defeated and divided by ten Barbarian tribes, what is now present-day Europe, into ten Roman countries today. They are:

- Alemanni: Germany

- Burgundians: Swiss

- Franks: French

- Lombard's: Italians

- Saxons: English

- Suevi: Portuguese

- Visigoth: Spanish

- Heruli: Extinct

- Ostrogoths: Extinct

- Vandals: Extinct

The iron nature of Rome will try to revive itself through men, as stated in prophecy. Daniel 2:43 *"As you saw iron mixed with ceramic clay, they will mingle with the seed of men; but they will not adhere to one another, just as iron does not mix with clay."*

Our history sadly has recorded events of those men who attempted to reunite the Roman Empire and failed every time. They are:

- King Charlemagne 768 -814 tried and failed

- King Charles V 1519-1556 tried and failed

- Louis XIV 1643-1715 tried and failed

- Napoleon Bonaparte 1804-1814 tried and failed

- Adolf Hitler 1934-1945 tried and failed

These men of human history tried to conquer the whole world and rule as the Romans once did but failed miserably; they committed great atrocities and caused even greater suffering in their efforts to achieve.

## Daniel's End-Time Vision

Daniel's end-time vision gives very little hope for the future of humanity and the church. His vision states that iron will mix with clay, and society will have the capacity to show great compassion and perform extraordinary acts of kindness while simultaneously being filled with rage, fury, hostility, and hatred that manifest themselves in passive-aggressive, aggressive, volatile, and abusive behaviors. We have seen these characteristics play out in our sordid history time and time again, especially among the three barbarian nations involved in the creation of the United States, England, France, and Italy. We come from volatile peoples and cannot seem to escape our ancestry. We find ourselves in this present-day quagmire of aggressive divisiveness and cultural war between ideologies, races, and classes. It is all motivated by people's fears of losing! Income, homes, jobs, and status in a heartless and sometimes barbaric capitalistic society that struggles to help its own. Here is where the church needs to be the clay and divorce itself from the iron that hinders its charity through greed and contempt and leaves us to lash out at and blame each other for the environmental woes of the day, like the skyrocketing crime rates and the economic flows of inflation, all the while failing to see our common humanity and common enemy, the one behind the veil who influences the mind and sets emotions a blaze. The very one the church has been called out to battle with on our behalf. For example, the middle class in America has long been the financial foundation of society. They fund our national and local governments, social programs, military and defense budgets, social security, and all salaries, expenses, and perks of the electorate. Yet still, they get very little help other than promised tax breaks that don't amount to any significant increase in annual income.

The apostle Paul wrote a very critical piece of information to the church in Ephesus about crucial thinking during war times and times of intense pressure.

He said this in Ephesians 6: 12-17 *"or we do not wrestle against flesh and blood, but against principalities, against powers, against the rulers of the darkness of this age, against spiritual hosts of wickedness in the heavenly places. Therefore take up the whole armor of God that you may be able to withstand in the evil day, and having done all, to stand. Stand therefore, having girded your waist with truth, having put on the breastplate of righteousness, and having shod your feet with the preparation of the gospel of peace; above all, taking the shield of faith with which you will be able to quench all the fiery darts of the wicked one. And take the helmet of salvation, and the sword of the Spirit, which is the word of God."*

Paul is shouting to us from the chronicle of time as a watchman on the wall to keep our heads and hold our peace and truly see the real enemy in the room; they are:

- Principalities: Rulers, Monarchies, Princes, Wealth, leaders with dark imaginations, and spiritual hosts of wickedness in heavenly places. Influential darkness that plays on the insecurities of the weak.

- Preparation: There is a dress code for success in this life that can't be bought at the designer store. This is spiritual clothing to protect from being tempted, enticed, or provoked. It starts with the truth around the waist, your center of gravity so doubt can't sway you off balance, a steal plate of righteousness to protect a righteous heart, shoes of peace to walk away from confusion and titillating gossip, a shield of faith to protect you from the darts of doubt, depression, discouragement, and disappear. A helmet of salvation to keep the message of the promise always on the forefront of the mind and the sword of the spirit, the Rhema and Logos word of God for the individual and the world.

The middle-class people feel they are abused the most as they watch the rich get richer and politicians lie without consciousness. The poor are manipulated by ones called "Black Lives Matter," "MAGA," and the "Alt-Right." Paul's message is for them to stop being spiritually enslaved and get liberated from toxic positivity and the love of money and be thy brother's keeper.

Even today in late 2022, the newly elected governor of the state of Virginia, "Glen Youngkin," is missing an opportunity to heal our broken land and his State by denying its history and how it will be taught in grades K through 12th grade. The governor's five newly appointed members to the school board have rejected the academically sound new curriculum that is revised every seven years according to Virginia law. We see toxic politics meddling in these affairs because of our national sin and our inability to address it once and for all. There is an ancient and wise saying, "Those who forget their history are doomed to repeat it." This the church cannot allow.

We have a choice for a different way ahead; even though the headwinds are strong, our vehicle is much stronger. The strength to choose this path will require trust and faith in God and abandoning our attachment to hate and brokenness as it relates to one another. In his first letter to the Corinthian church, the apostle Paul spoke to them, addressing the root of their sin. His message dealt with the narcissistic nature of sin and its weakness when confronted by the power of love. He said, "*If I speak in the tongues of men or angels but do not have love, I am only a resounding gong or a clanging cymbal. If I have the gift of prophecy and can fathom all mysteries and all knowledge, and if I have a faith that can move mountains but do not have love, I am nothing. If I give all I possess to the poor and give over my body to hardship that I may boast but do not have love, I gain nothing. Love is patient; love is kind. It does not envy; it does not boast; it is not proud. It does not dishonor others; it is not self-seeking; it is not easily angered; it keeps no record of wrongs. Love does not delight in evil but rejoices with the truth. It always protects, always trusts, hopes, and always perseveres. Love never fails. But where there are prophecies, they will cease; where there are tongues, they will be stilled; where there is knowledge, it will pass away."*

The power of love is for the oppressor and the oppressed; we find ourselves in this point-counterpoint existence which manifests itself through the regurgitation of past pains of our national sin and justifications for current behaviors. Jesus Christ tells his church in the 18th chapter of the book of Matthew, *"that whatever you bind on earth will be bound in heaven and whatever you loose on earth will be loosed in heaven."* With Christ, every aspect of human relationships is about grace and reconciliation. So, in the realm of relationships binding and loosing can be forbidding or permitting or, even better, convicting or acquitting. We, the individual, must make this daily decision to forgive and pardon or not forgive and condemn in our hearts.

So, as I conclude the journey towards American Christianity through American and world history, my goal has been to find and identify a specific character in our spiritual genome that can make some sense for the centuries of atrocities, pain, and suffering we have burdened each other with, in the name of progress, profit, and politics. We traveled to the sugarcane plantations of the Caribbean, the American south during its darkest periods, and even the Church of Rome.

Finally, in our present time and space, we find ourselves. This journey has revealed the concept of institutional evil, birthed out of privilege, entitlement, and zero accountability. This comes from a small segment of people being in charge for too long and creating systems that allow benefits not afforded to most. It has become a way of expected living in the world, and the more people who believe in it and feel entitled to it, the more hell they are willing to raise to possess it.

In conclusion, our future is hopeful because our path is clear. We have no choice but to resist the winds of inner temptations, seek higher plains of communication in our relationships, and allow the power of love to dull the aggression, mistrust, and ill will we carry in our hearts. As we travel this new path, I leave you this advice from Ephesians 5:15-17 "<u>See then that you walk circumspectly, not as fools but as wise, redeeming the time, because the days are evil. Therefore, do not be unwise, but understand the will of the Lord.</u>"

# OTHER BOOKS BY
# PASTOR OWEN WILLIAMS

- The Corporate Christian: Christian Beliefs vs. Corporate Behaviors

- The Corporate Christian 2: Battle for your Beliefs

- The Corporate Christian 3: The Hidden War

# BIBLIOGRAPHY

Noll, A. Mark. Turning Points Decisive Moments in the History of Christianity. Grand Rapid, MI, Baker Academic, 2012

Priscilla Papers Academic Journal. Winter 2000. Scripture and Race

Vischer, Robert K. (2001). ." Florida Law Review. 53: 193

Winter D. Ralph, Hawthorne C. Steven. Perspective on the World›s Christian Movement. Pasadena Ca, William Carey Library, 2009

Clinton, Tim, Hawkins, Ron. The Quick Reference Guide to Biblical Counseling Personal and Emotional issues, Baker Books, 2009.

Rothstein, Richard. The Color of Law, Liveright Publishing Corporation, 2017.

Milestone Documents. National Archives 02/08/2022

# MORE ABOUT PASTOR WILLIAMS

Pastor Owen E. Williams is the Pastor of the St. Mark Missionary Baptist church. Where he has served as senior pastor for the last Seventeen years, he is also the retired Director of Pastoral Care Services at the New York City Health and Hospitals Corporation Kings County Hospital. There he oversaw the spiritual care for the seven-hundred-bed public hospital. Pastor Williams has a master's degree in Pastoral Counseling, an Honorary Doctorate in Divinity, and a bachelor's degree in Criminal Justice. He is the author of three published books (**The Corporate Christian: Christian Beliefs Vs. Corporate Behaviors, The Corporate Christian 2: The Battle for your Beliefs, and The Corporate Christian 3: The Hidden War**), the President of the Queens Federation of Churches Board of Directors, former NYPD clergy liaison for the 103rd Precinct, a former member of the Board of Directors for Live on NY the second largest OPO (Organ Procurement Organization) in North America and the founder and President of OE Williams Ministries. Pastor Williams frequently travels to Johannesburg, South Africa, where he conducts training seminars on Solution Focus Pastoral Counseling for social workers, schoolteachers, police officers, and clergy. Pastor Williams has been married to Elder Debora Williams, his wife, for over 32 years, and they have one daughter Desiree Rose Williams. Throughout Pastor Williams' Christian journey, the Lord has taught him many things, but two things have always stayed with him; maximize your moments, we have so few, and an ounce of practice is worth a ton of preaching. Let us all be practitioners rather than preachers of the gospel, doers rather than hear of the word.